Microwave Magic
Desserts II

Grolier Limited
TORONTO

Contributors to this series:

Recipes and Technical Assistance:
École de cuisine Bachand-Bissonnette
Cooking consultants:
Denis Bissonette
Michèle Émond
Dietician:
Christiane Barbeau
Photos:
Laramée Morel Communications
Audio-Visuelles
Design:
Claudette Taillefer
Assistants:
Julie Deslauriers
Philippe O'Connor
Joan Pothier
Accessories:
Andrée Cournoyer
Writing:
Communications La Griffe Inc.
Text Consultants:
Cap et bc inc.
Advisors:
Roger Aubin
Joseph R. De Varennes
Gaston Lavoie
Kenneth H. Pearson

Assembly:
Carole Garon
Vital Lapalme
Jean-Pierre Larose
Carl Simmons
Gus Soriano
Marc Vallières
Production Managers:
Gilles Chamberland
Ernest Homewood
Production Assistants:
Martine Gingras
Catherine Gordon
Kathy Kishimoto
Peter Thomlison
Art Director:
Bernard Lamy
Editors:
Laurielle Ilacqua
Susan Marshall
Margaret Oliver
Robin Rivers
Lois Rock
Jocelyn Smyth
Donna Thomson
Dolores Williams
Development:
Le Groupe Polygone Éditeurs Inc.

We wish to thank the following firms, PIER I IMPORTS and LE CACHE POT, for their contribution to the illustration of this set.

The series editors have taken every care to ensure that the information given is accurate. However, no cookbook can guarantee the user successful results. The editors cannot accept any responsibility for the results obtained by following the recipes and recommendations given.

Canadian Cataloguing in Publication Data

Main entry under title:

Desserts II

(Microwave magic ; 9)
Translation of: Les Desserts II.
Includes index.
ISBN 0-7172-2430-9

1. Desserts.   2. Microwave cookery.
I. Series: Microwave magic (Toronto, Ont.) ; 9.

TX832.D3913 1988   641.8'68   C88-094208-8

Contents

Microwave Magic is a multi-volume set, with each volume devoted to a particular type of cooking. So, if you are looking for a chicken recipe, you simply go to one of the two volumes that deal with poultry. Each volume has its own index, and the final volume contains a general index to the complete set.

Microwave Magic puts over twelve hundred recipes at your fingertips. You will find it as useful as the microwave oven itself. Enjoy!

Note from the Editor

How to Use this Book
The books in this set have been designed to make your job as easy as possible. As a result, most of the recipes are set out in a standard way.

We suggest that you begin by consulting the information chart for the recipe you have chosen. You will find there all the information you need to decide if you are able to make it: preparation time, cost per serving, level of difficulty, number of calories per serving and other relevant details. Thus, if you have only 30 minutes in which to prepare the evening meal, you will quickly be able to tell which recipe is possible and suits your schedule.

The list of ingredients is always clearly separated from the main text. When space allows, the ingredients are shown together in a photograph so that you can make sure you have them all without rereading the list—another way of saving your **valuable time. In addition, for the more complex recipes we have supplied photographs of the key stages involved either in preparation or serving.**

All the dishes in this book have been cooked in a 700 watt microwave oven. If your oven has a different wattage, consult the conversion chart that appears on the following page for cooking times in different types of oven. We would like to emphasize that the cooking times given in the book are a minimum. If a dish does not seem to be cooked enough, you may return it to the oven for a few more minutes. Also, the cooking time can vary according to your ingredients: their water and fat content, thickness, shape and even where they come from. We have therefore left a blank space on each recipe page in which you can note the cooking time that suits you best. This will enable you to add a personal touch to the recipes that we suggest and to reproduce your best results every time.

Although we have put all the technical information together at the front of this book, we have inserted a number of boxed entries called **MICROTIPS** throughout to explain particular techniques. They are brief and simple, and will help you obtain successful results in your cooking.

With the very first recipe you try, you will discover just how simple microwave cooking can be and how often it depends on techniques you already use for cooking with a conventional oven. If cooking is a pleasure for you, as it is for us, it will be all the more so with a microwave oven. Now let's get on with the food.

The Editor

Key to the Symbols
For ease of reference, the following symbols have been used on the recipe information charts.

The pencil symbol is a reminder to write your cooking time in the space provided.

Level of Difficulty

Easy

Moderate

Complex

Cost per Serving

$ Inexpensive

$ $ Moderate

$ $ $ Expensive

Power Levels

All the recipes in this book have been tested in a 700 watt oven. As there are many microwave ovens on the market with different power levels, and as the names of these levels vary from one manufacturer to another, we have decided to give power levels as a percentage. To adapt the power levels given here, consult the chart opposite and the instruction manual for your oven.

Generally speaking, if you have a 500 watt or 600 watt oven you should increase cooking times by about 30% over those given, depending on the actual length of time required. The shorter the original cooking time, the greater the percentage by which it must be lengthened. The 30% figure is only an average. Consult the chart for detailed information on this topic.

Power Levels

HIGH: 100% - 90%	Vegetables (except boiled potatoes and carrots) Soup Sauce Fruits Browning ground beef Browning dish Popcorn
MEDIUM HIGH: 80% - 70%	Rapid defrosting of precooked dishes Muffins Some cakes Hot dogs
MEDIUM: 60% - 50%	Cooking tender meat Cakes Fish Seafood Eggs Reheating Boiled potatoes and carrots
MEDIUM LOW: 40%	Cooking less tender meat Simmering Melting chocolate
DEFROST: 30% **LOW: 30% - 20%**	Defrosting Simmering Cooking less tender meat
WARM: 10%	Keeping food warm Allowing yeast dough to rise

Cooking Time Conversion Chart

700 watts	600 watts*
5 s	11 s
15 s	20 s
30 s	40 s
45 s	1 min
1 min	1 min 20 s
2 min	2 min 40 s
3 min	4 min
4 min	5 min 20 s
5 min	6 min 40 s
6 min	8 min
7 min	9 min 20 s
8 min	10 min 40 s
9 min	12 min
10 min	13 min 30 s
20 min	26 min 40 s
30 min	40 min
40 min	53 min 40 s
50 min	66 min 40 s
1 h	1 h 20 min

* There is very little difference in cooking times between 500 watt ovens and 600 watt ovens.

Happy Endings

"If you don't finish your supper, you won't get any dessert!" How many times in our childhood has that phrase been used to hurry us through our meals to get to dessert. As children become adults, they manage their appetites so that they can pace their eating and "save a little spot" for dessert.

Children and adults alike find desserts attractive and appetizing. Desserts mean parties, celebrations and rewards.

At family get-togethers, the dessert course is the time for laughter and amusement. During the meal, guests have enjoyed a series of elaborate dishes and have helped themselves generously to both food and wine. By now everyone is lively and the conversation flows. At this moment, dessert is brought to the table. If the dessert is even simply decorated, the reactions will be immediate: general exclamations, flattering comments, applause and pressing requests from the children. The dessert has worked its

magical effect and guests will remember this meal for a long time.

For a business meal, things are a little different. In this case, as we know, the quality of the dishes usually goes unnoticed. But the discussions have been successful and a general agreement has been reached. The atmosphere begins to lighten just as the dessert is brought to the table. Then the smiles are more frequent, the jokes begin and the conversation slowly moves to more personal topics. Without quite knowing why, the mood becomes more comfortable. Coincidentally the dessert is delicious and beautifully decorated.

In fact, desserts play an important role in all the happy occasions of our lives.

Cakes and pastries form the largest category of desserts. This is probably because the secret of pastry making was discovered so long ago, and the idea of sweetening its taste, first with honey and later with cane sugar, rapidly

followed.

Fruits are often neglected but they make naturally beautiful desserts. They can be lightly poached, cooked in a compote, served individually or mixed with other ingredients. They make attractive salads, surprising decorations or garnishes, syrups or sauces. Fruits give desserts a distinctive flavor.

Other recipes add imagination to the chapter on sweet dishes. Puddings deliciously combine a batter, a cereal or semolina and a sweet sauce. Mousses, generally smothered with sauce or elegantly decorated, combine lightness with exquisite flavor.

The time spent preparing desserts is never wasted. This last part of a meal is not any less important than the preceding courses; everyone looks forward to dessert, even if the main dish is much appreciated and plentiful. And if you ever contemplate not serving dessert, think about the happy excited glow that will be missing in the eyes of children of all ages.

Desserts: A Love Match of Art and Technique

Cooking is an art which produces satisfactory results only when its own set of basic techniques is correctly applied. Simple but rigorous rules govern the proper selection of ingredients, the precise measurement of quantities, the methods of preparation and the choice of utensils for mixing and cooking.

Basic Ingredients: Sugar, Flour, Yeasts and Fruits

Sugar — long linked with desserts — is the natural product of plants such as sugar cane and fruits, and is an essential element of a balanced diet. The sugars used in the preparation of desserts belong to one of five major commercial categories; icing sugar, white granulated sugar, sugar candy, fruit sugar, and brown sugar, which may be refined or unrefined.

It is recommended that you do not substitute syrup, molasses or honey for the type of sugar specified in a recipe. You may replace white sugar with brown sugar but remember: brown sugar requires a longer cooking time.

White flour is produced in various ways which affect the uses to which it will be put. There are five different types of white flour: all purpose, enriched, pastry, cake and self-raising. Self-raising flour contains salt and two types of raising agents: baking soda and baking powder.

Raising agents, by giving off a colorless, odorless gas, cause dough or batter to rise; without these agents the dough would remain heavy and hard to digest. Three raising agents, baking soda, baking powder and cream of tartar, are interchangeably used in some recipes. There are several types of yeast available; the most commonly used are fresh yeast, dried yeast and chemical yeasts.

An incredible number of ingredients may be used as principal ingredients in the preparation of a dessert; syrups, creams, sweet preparations such as caramel or chocolate, or even vegetables. However, fruits continue to be a favorite of dessert lovers. Fruits can be used in so many different ways: fresh or dry, in jams or in syrups. They offer a wide variety of tastes and combine well with nuts or spices to produce a delicious flavor.

Measuring Ingredients

It may seem unnecessary to attach so much importance to such a simple thing as measuring ingredients. However, even small variations in quantities often have a very serious effect on the taste of the final product and may make the difference between a successful recipe and a disastrous disappointment. It is necessary to pay close attention to the measurement of all ingredients. To measure liquid and powdered ingredients, the best utensil is a transparent measuring cup with a proper rim and a pouring lip. To measure accurately, set the cup on a flat surface and check at eye level that the ingredient is

 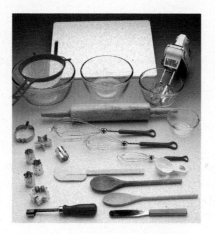 

right on the mark. The rim and pouring lip will ensure that liquids can be poured properly.

Many dry ingredients measure differently depending on whether or not they are packed down. It is recommended that ingredients such as flour and baking powder be leveled off with a knife or spatula. Ingredients such as brown sugar should be packed down. All the dry ingredients in this book are measured in this way.

Fats such as margarine, lard or shortening are easy to measure if you first pour 125 mL (1/2 cup) of cold water into a measuring cup and then immerse the fat into the water until the water level reaches the desired quantity of fat plus 125 mL (1/2 cup).

Different sizes of eggs are available; they can be small, medium, large or extra-large. The recipes in this book are all prepared with large eggs. If this size of egg is not available adjust the required quantity, bearing in mind that one large egg corresponds to about 50 mL (1/4 cup).

Cooking Utensils for the Preparation of Desserts

The first category of cooking utensils includes those used for measuring. Other than the measuring cup, already mentioned above, the utensils considered indispensable include a set of standard measuring spoons in both the metric (international) system and the imperial system. The measuring cup should also have both metric and imperial measurements. Ordinary kitchen utensils (such as teaspoons, tablespoons, cups, etc.) are not uniform in size and should never be substituted for accurate measuring utensils.

A second category of utensils is that used for mixing, kneading, cutting, beating, etc. A basic set includes mixing bowls, two sieves, a rolling pin, a whisk, an electric mixer, spatulas, spoons, a pastry knife, etc.

Nuts and Coconuts for Delicious Desserts

The last category is made up of baking pans and dishes. Most non-metallic baking pans or dishes are suitable for microwave cooking. However we recommend that you use round, transparent dishes which better distribute the microwave energy and allow you to check for doneness by a simple visual inspection.

Nuts and Coconuts for Delicious Desserts

The term *nut* has come to include everything from coconuts to hazelnuts. All contain significant quantities of polyunsaturated fats and are therefore sometimes called oliaginous fruits. Nuts are a popular cooking ingredient because of their wide variety of rich tastes. They are particularly popular in desserts as an important ingredient or as a garnish for pastries, puddings and other desserts. This decorative use ranges from arranging pecans on a tart to making a delicate pattern of hazelnuts on the icing of a cake. Grated coconut is also often used to garnish or cover cookies and small cakes.

The nuts in many desserts are not always visible. They may be chopped finely, ground or grated and then combined with other ingredients. But they do not pass unobserved, revealing to the discriminating palate all their exquisite sweetness. Hazelnuts may be grilled, peeled and ground; likewise, ground almonds may be mixed with sugar and eggs to make a savory almond paste. Almonds may also be added to sugar and the sugar caramelized to make a fine praline. Walnuts and pecans, coarsely chopped, are a delicious addition to cakes and cookies.

As well as offering a variety of incomparable flavors, nuts are extremely nutritious and many of them contain significant proportions of elements essential to a balanced diet (magnesium for example) which are difficult to find in other foods. They contain between 10% and 25% protein and are high in fiber and vitamins such as thiamin, riboflavin and Vitamin E. The small table below will give you an idea of the amount of nutritional elements contained in some of the most popular nuts.

It's easy to see that the use of nuts in recipes is not limited to an eye- and palate-pleasing function. It is rare that a food is flavorful, decorative — and nutritious.

The Nutritional Value of Some Nuts

Nut	Quantity mL/cup	Cal.	Calcium mg	Iron mg	Potassium mg
Almonds	125/½	449	175	4.0	580
Brazil Nuts	125/½	451	128	2.3	493
Cashews	125/½	415	28	2.8	343
Coconuts	125/½	183	14	1.1	194
Peanuts	125/½	438	56	1.4	506
Pecans	125/½	392	42	1.4	344
Walnuts	125/½	345	52	1.6	239

Source: Health and Welfare Canada, *Nutrient Value of Some Common Foods* (1979)

Spices and Flavorings:
From the Succulent to the Exquisite

Spices

Spice cookies, spice cakes, spice breads, gingerbread men. These names evoke warm memories for most of us. In fact, spices have played an important role in dessert preparation for a very long time.

The spices used in Western confectionary traditions are the ones most recently introduced to Europe. Nutmeg, ginger, cinnamon and cloves were discovered by Europeans at the time of the Crusades. Today, could we imagine an apple pie without cinnamon? Certainly not, judging from the number of recipes for apple fillings all made with this popular spice. Ground cinnamon is also used in spice breads.

Cardamom is less widely used, but can be found in several cake recipes. It is used in combination with other spices.

Cloves can be used whole or crushed. Whole, they are used for decoration and to add flavor to fruit compotes. Crushed, they are used most notably in seasoning spice breads. Ginger — another spice — is a root that can easily be found fresh or powdered to flavor various batters.

Like cinnamon, nutmeg adds an interesting flavor to apples. Grated, it is used in garnishes, compotes, spice breads and cakes. Pepper is often neglected but is used in many different confections. Its rather pronounced flavor adds character to other recipes.

Of course salt is not a spice but it does play an essential role in the chemistry of doughs and batters.

Flavorings

In addition to the better known spices, some other flavorings deserve mention and are an important part of dessert preparation. Among these flavorings, the most commonly used are lemon rind, orange rind, fruit sugars and vanilla.

Candied lemon rind is often used as part of a dried fruit garnish to decorate light cakes such as cream cheese cakes. Lemon zest adds flavor to innumerable preparations. It is added to tart garnishes, meringues and to some cooked pastry creams. Grated lemon rind is also used to add flavor to petits fours made with genoese cake.

Candied orange rind is used in much the same way as the lemon rind: as a dried fruit garnish or a garnish for cookies. Chopped orange zest can be sprinkled on small cakes just before cooking. Finely grated orange rind can be added to meringues.

The fruit of the vanilla tree, unlike that of the lemon or orange, is sought for neither its flesh nor its skin. Only the extract of vanilla is used in pastry making. This product is obtained by boiling the ripe fruit and drying it so that it becomes covered with vanilla crystals, which give the vanilla extract its distinctive flavor. Vanilla extract is sold in powder and in liquid form.

The list of spices and flavorings we have drawn up here is not exhaustive. There are many other tastes to be experienced as you discover new desserts.

Adapting Recipes

Must you throw out all your conventional recipes when you install a microwave oven? Of course not! On the contrary, most conventional recipes can easily be adapted for use in the microwave. To do this, however, you must keep in mind a few basic principles on microwave cooking and how it differs from conventional cooking.

On your first attempt to adapt a recipe to the microwave oven, be sure to choose one that you know well. It will be much easier to work out the changes that are required if you know what the final result should be. If you want to adapt a recipe with which you are not familiar, try to assess whether or not it is likely to give the result you want. If a particular dish is not to your liking when prepared in the conventional way, it is not likely to appeal to you any more when cooked in the microwave oven.

Remember that, contrary to what you may have heard, most conventional recipes can be adapted to the microwave without altering the list of ingredients or the method of preparation. Sometimes only minor changes need to be made, as in the recipe shown on the right. In these cases, the microwave oven offers the tremendous advantage of considerably reducing the cooking time without requiring any major changes to the original recipe.

Basic Principles for Adapting Recipes

Ingredients: Liquid ingredients slow down microwave cooking whereas fat ingredients speed it up. To adapt a conventional recipe you must reduce the amount of liquid and fat to obtain the right balance between the two. Never include more than 75 mL (1/3 cup) of oil in a microwave recipe. If a recipe lists more than this amount, use only 75 mL (1/3 cup).

In the same way, the quantity of water required in a traditional recipe will normally be reduced by 20% to 25%. In the recipe shown on the right, and in most other dessert recipes it is not necessary to alter the list of ingredients.

Method: To ensure even cooking, you must give the dish or container a half-turn during the cooking period. In order to know when and how often to do this, find a recipe similar to the one you are adapting and follow the instructions given for this procedure. In the recipe shown on the right, the cakes are cooked separately and each dish is given a half-turn after 4 minutes of cooking time.

Cooking Time: In this respect, the advantage of the microwave oven is clear and will certainly encourage you to adapt many of your conventional recipes. In our recipe for Chocolate Fudge Cake, the cooking time is reduced from 50 or 60 minutes to 16 minutes, that is 8 minutes per cake.

Utensils: Never use any bowl or container that is made of metal or has a metal rim in the microwave oven. However, you can use bowls, dishes and plates made of heat-resistant glass or plastic. You probably have a wide range of suitable containers in your kitchen cupboards and should therefore check to see if you have the right one for a given recipe before buying a new one for that specific purpose.

Chocolate Fudge Cake— Conventional Recipe*

Ingredients
125 mL (1/2 cup) butter
5 mL (1 teaspoon) vanilla
500 mL (2 cups) sugar
2 eggs
650 mL (2-2/3 cups) flour
2 mL (1/2 teaspoon) salt
10 mL (2 teaspoons) baking soda
125 mL (1/2 cup) cocoa
500 mL (2 cups) sour milk

Method
— Cream the butter, then slowly add the vanilla and sugar. Continue beating until smooth and light.
— In another bowl, beat the eggs, add to the butter mixture.
— Sift the flour, salt, baking soda and cocoa 4 or 5 times.
— Add the dry ingredients to the butter mixture alternately with the milk. Begin and end with the dry ingredients.
— **Grease the inside of two round cake pans and pour half the batter into each.**
— **Place the cakes in the middle of the oven and cook at 180°C (350°F) for 50-60 minutes.** Insert a toothpick to test for doneness. Continue cooking if necessary.
— Let stand on a rack for 5 to 10 minutes before turning out.

*Steps needing modifying are indicated in bold type.

Chocolate Fudge Cake— Recipe Adapted For Microwave Cooking*

Ingredients
125 mL (1/2 cup) butter
5 mL (1 teaspoon) vanilla
500 mL (2 cups) sugar
2 eggs
650 mL (2-2/3 cups) flour
2 mL (1/2 teaspoon) salt
10 mL (2 teaspoons) baking soda
125 mL (1/2 cup) cocoa
500 mL (2 cups) sour milk

Method
— Cream the butter, then slowly add the vanilla and sugar. Continue beating until smooth and light.
— In another bowl, beat the eggs; add to the butter mixture.
— Sift the flour, salt, baking soda and cocoa 4 or 5 times.
— Add the dry ingredients to the butter mixture alternately with the milk. Begin and end with the dry ingredients.
— **Line the bottom of two round cake pans with waxed paper** and pour half the batter in each.
— **Cook each of the cakes spearately on a raised rack at 70% for 4 minutes. Give the dish a half-turn and continue cooking for 4 minutes.** Insert a toothpick to test for doneness. Continue cooking if necessary.
— **Cook the second cake in the same way.**
— Let stand for 5 to 10 minutes on a rack before turning out.

*Modifications are indicated in bold type.

Great Classic Desserts

Desserts are much like musical pieces; some don't survive their opening night, others have a longer life but eventually fade away. Those which survive the test of time are considered masterpieces. People have been making desserts since the age of the Pharaohs, so it is easy to imagine that many of these sweet works have passed into the annals of history. Here we have provided a brief list of some of the great classic desserts to demonstrate how the history of nations has left some very appetizing traces.

Candied Angelica
Angelica is a herb introduced into France by the Vikings. Its green stalks are candied and frequently used to decorate pastries.

Rum Baba
The baba's invention is attributed to a Polish king exiled in France, whose favorite hero was Ali Baba. It's a rather exotic background for a pastry, but whether the story is true or not, the baba is a small individual cake made of leavened dough and soaked in rum (or Kirsch) after cooking. Raisins are traditionally added to the dough.

Bavarian Cream
The texture of a Bavarian Cream is much like that of a Crème Caramel. It is made by combining English custard or a fruit purée with gelatin or whipped cream. It is placed in a mold and served chilled.

Clafoutis
This dessert originated in the Limousin area of France. A traditional clafoutis is prepared by pouring a thick pancake-like batter over a layer of black cherries in a buttered dish. The mixture is then cooked in the oven.

Sugar Tart
How could we not include, in the list of well-known desserts, our own national favorite, also well known outside the country? Our much-loved sugar tart deserves to be included in the ranks of the classics.

Fruit Compote
The compote, especially one made from a mixture of fruits, has been renowned for a long time. There is an endless variety of fruit combinations, all of which produce lovely syrups.

Charlotte Russe
The classic version of the charlotte is flavored with strawberries and served cold, but the charlotte may also be prepared with raspberries, apples and other fruits. A form of mousse, the charlotte is poured into a mold whose bottom and sides are lined with sponge fingers.

Chocolate Eclair
This puff pastry dessert is so well known that no description is necessary. Only the filling remains a mystery. It can be filled with Chantilly cream, pastry cream, chocolate, coffee or chestnut cream.

Angel Cake
Made with stiffly beaten egg whites flavored with vanilla or almond essence, this cake owes its name to its very light consistency. It is so delicious

it needs no filling or frosting.

Black Forest Cake

A very well known and very popular cake, it is often just called a Black Forest. This classic cake may be decorated in many ways, but the basic ingredients are the same: a rich chocolate batter flavored with kirsch, Chantilly cream, liqueur-soaked cherries and chocolate shavings.

Mille-Feuille

This dessert is made with thin layers of flaky pastry separated by layers of cream and covered with a marbled icing. The pastry cream or Chantilly cream filling is sometimes flavored with rum or kirsch.

Chocolate Mousse

There are many different ways of preparing chocolate mousse. Most recipes call for eggs, whipped cream and, of course, chocolate, combined to produce a smooth and silky dessert.

Brownies

Since Brownies are a classic North American dessert, everyone has surely tasted them at some time. They are made of a very thick chocolate-based batter.

Paris-Brest

At the end of the nineteenth century, a French pastry chef invented this pastry to celebrate, in his own way, the bicycle race between Paris and Brest. The dessert was originally made in the form of a bicycle wheel. Nowadays, it is made of a crown of flaky pastry, stuffed with praline butter cream and decorated with almonds and icing sugar.

Peaches Cardinal

This dessert owes its name to its beautiful red, almost purple colored sauce. The dessert is made by poaching peach halves in a vanilla syrup, then sprinkling them with a raspberry sauce and garnishing with a Chantilly cream.

Profiteroles

This dessert is made of little balls of choux pastry which are stuffed with either pastry cream, Chantilly cream, ice cream or jam. The balls are then arranged in dishes and covered with chocolate sauce. Savory profiteroles may be stuffed with cream cheese, game purée, etc.

Savarin

Made of the same leavened dough as the rum baba, the savarin cake is cooked in a ring mold and sprinkled with a rum flavored sugar syrup. The cake is then decorated with pastry cream or Chantilly cream and fruit.

The Brioche: A Name with a Million Flavors

The word brioche refers to pastries of many different shapes, sizes and textures which makes it difficult to give an exact definition.

Even the origin of the word brioche remains somewhat obscure; does the term originate from the area of Brie? Did the original recipe use Brie cheese? The name may have been formed from the words Brie and *hocher*, the latter meaning to stir. Many dictionaries agree that the word was formed from the Old Norman verb *brier* meaning to break. But now let us move from the search for the geographic origin of the pastry to investigate what it is that makes these Norman brioches so popular.

What does the word brioche now mean? It is a light, fluffy pastry made from a yeast dough. The proportion of butter and eggs may vary from one recipe to the next, which will alter the consistency of the pastry. This is not a very precise definition, but since the term includes such a wide variety of sweet buns it is impossible to be more precise.

The brioche dough is made by mixing butter, water or milk, flour, yeast, eggs and sugar. In one variation the yeast is replaced by beer to make the dough even lighter.

The brioche is made differently according to regional traditions. The crown-shaped brioche, used to make the Twelfth-Night Cake, originated in Europe. Among the most well-known brioches are the mousseline brioche from France, in the shape of a tall cylinder; the Nanterre brioche, with sharp angles and the Parisian brioche, with two balls of dough, one on top of the other. Many French people begin their day with a brioche and a cup of coffee, milk or hot chocolate.

Elsewhere, different kinds of brioche are made, some more refined than others. They are also made for special celebrations, sometimes to commemorate the birth of a patron saint, or to celebrate a village wedding. The most famous of these is the incredible Vendean bride's wedding cake which is known to have been made 1.3 metres (51 inches) in diameter. Closer to home, some small English buns are considered to be brioches. A brioche is usually made from small pieces of dough put together so that they attach during cooking time. It may be filled and glazed. Another type of brioche is made of spiral-shaped pastry dough, flavored with cinnamon, garnished with dried raisins and glazed. As well as these basic North American types, many other commercial varieties can be found.

The brioche is not just a dessert. It can be baked with no special flavoring and used as a crust for beef, liver or sausage fillings. However, here we shall consider the dessert brioche, stuffed with fruit or cream.

Making Quick Breads

Quick Breads are so universally appreciated that all you need to do is bring a hot loaf to the table to be rewarded with smiles all around. Whether it's a small bun eaten on the run for breakfast or for a daily snack or a large, festive ring which decorates the table and is shared with guests on special occasions, the success of this type of pastry depends on the care taken in preparing the dough. We hope that you will find these few suggestions helpful.

Why Not Keep Extra Dough On Hand?
You may find that you have just enough time to cook some buns, but not enough time to prepare the dough. Why not prepare some partially-made dough in advance and keep it in the freezer? Then, when needed, just add egg, vanilla, milk and cook.

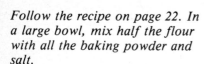

Follow the recipe on page 22. In a large bowl, mix half the flour with all the baking powder and salt.

Add the sugar and vegetable oil and beat at medium speed until the mixture becomes grainy. Add the remaining flour and beat until thoroughly combined.

Place the mixture in a tightly sealed container and label and date it. Freeze. The mixture will keep for 4 to 5 weeks.

MICROTIPS

To Melt Chocolate
Cakes, pastries or ice cream will all taste better covered with melted chocolate. The microwave oven lets you melt chocolate without using a double boiler. Put the chocolate pieces in a microwave-safe dish with a small amount of fat and heat at 50% for 1 to 2 minutes.

MICROTIPS

Success with Bread

Here are some practical tips which will help you with leavened bread recipes. To obtain a more flavorful bread and to promote the action of the yeast, add a small amount of sweetener such as white sugar, molasses, brown sugar or honey to the dough.

The water should be between 41°C and 46°C (105°F and 115°F). A higher temperature will destroy the yeast and prevent the bread from rising.

The less flour used, the better the bread will be. Don't necessarily use all the flour indicated in a recipe. Once the dough no longer feels sticky, stop adding flour.

Room temperatures will affect the rising action of the yeast. In a warm spot, bread will rise in just two hours. However, the bread will have a more delicate taste if it rises more slowly. It is therefore recommended that the dough be left to rise in a cool place for 4 to 5 hours, or overnight in the refrigerator.

Success with Quick Breads

Here are some practical tips to help you make Quick Breads or to improve your own recipe. Quick Breads cook best in glass loaf pans. Choose a deep pan with straight sides. Pans designed for meatloaf are not large enough for this type of recipe. To make the bread easier to turn out, line the bottom of the pan with a piece of waxed paper.

If nuts or dried fruits are added to the dough, chop them very finely so that the pieces don't end up at the bottom of the pan during cooking. Protect the edges of the bread by covering the two ends of the pan with aluminum foil.

Give the dish a half-turn several times as the bread cooks. While turning the dish, check for doneness. Cooking is completed when no uncooked dough is visible at the center of the pan when viewed from below. Another way of checking for doneness is by inserting a toothpick into the bread; when it comes out clean and dry the bread is properly cooked.

Let the bread stand for 10 minutes, then turn out. Remove the waxed paper and let cool completely before slicing. This will prevent the bread from crumbling when sliced.

Quick Bread Dough

Ingredients
300 mL (1-1/4 cup) flour
10 mL (2 teaspoons) baking powder
2 mL (1/2 teaspoon) salt
150 mL (2/3 cup) sugar
30 mL (2 tablespoons) vegetable oil
1 egg
5 mL (1 teaspoon) vanilla
150 mL (2/3 cup) milk

Method
— Combine the flour, baking powder and salt; set aside.
— In a bowl, combine the sugar and oil, stirring until the mixture is smooth; add the egg and vanilla.
— Beat until the mixture becomes light.
— Gradually add the dry ingredients, alternately with the milk.
— Shape the dough according to directions given in the following recipes.

Quick Bread Ring with Nuts and Green Cherries

Ingredients
1 Quick Bread dough recipe, page 22
125 mL (1/2 cup) brown sugar
125 mL (1/2 cup) chopped nuts
5 mL (1 teaspoon) cinnamon
45 mL (3 tablespoons) butter
12 green candied cherries, cut in half

Method
— Combine the brown sugar, nuts and cinnamon; set aside.
— Beat the butter until smooth and add to the dry ingredients.
— Arrange the cherries at the bottom of a tube pan sprayed with an anti-stick agent, such as Pam.
— Sprinkle with the sugar mixture, then spoon in half the prepared dough.
— Cover with another layer of sugar mixture, and spoon in the remaining dough.
— Place the pan on a raised rack and cook at 70% for 8 to 10 minutes, giving the dish a half-turn halfway through cooking time.
— Let stand for 2 minutes, then turn out onto a serving platter.
— Let stand for another 2 minutes before serving.

Pineapple and Honey Ring

Ingredients
1 Quick Bread dough recipe,
page 22
45 mL (3 tablespoons) melted
butter
75 mL (1/3 cup) honey
75 mL (1/3 cup) grated
coconut
250 mL (1 cup) crushed
pineapple, drained

Method
— Combine the melted
butter and honey; set
aside.
— Sprinkle the grated
coconut on the bottom of
a tube pan sprayed with
an anti-stick agent, such
as Pam.
— Spoon in the pineapple,
then cover with the butter
and honey mixture.

— Top with the prepared
dough.
— Place the pan on a raised
rack and cook at 70% for
8 to 10 minutes, giving the
dish a half-turn halfway
through cooking time.
— Let stand for 2 minutes,
then turn out onto a
serving platter.
— Let stand another 2
minutes before serving.

24

Apple Quick Bread

Ingredients
1 Quick Bread dough recipe, page 22
2 medium apples
125 mL (1/2 cup) brown sugar
5 mL (1 teaspoon) cinnamon
45 mL (3 tablespoons) melted butter
50 mL (1/4 cup) chopped nuts

Method
— Core, peel and cut the apples into thin slices.
— Combine the brown sugar, cinnamon and melted butter; set aside.
— Arrange the apple slices on the bottom of a 20 cm (8 in) square pan.
— Sprinkle with half the sugar mixture.
— Spread half the prepared dough evenly on top, then sprinkle with the remaining sugar mixture.
— Sprinkle with nuts, then cover with the remaining dough.
— Place the pan on a raised rack and cook at 70% for 8 to 10 minutes, covering the four sides with a piece of aluminum foil during the first 5 minutes of cooking and giving the dish a half-turn halfway through cooking time.
— Let stand for 2 minutes, then turn out onto a serving platter.
— Let stand for another 2 minutes before serving.

Breakfast Buns

Level of Difficulty	🍴🍴
Preparation Time	20 min
Cost per Serving	$ $
Yield	12
Cooking Time	8 min
Standing Time	4 min
Power Level	70%
Write Your Cooking Time Here	

Ingredients
125 mL (1/2 cup) brown sugar
50 mL (1/4 cup) chopped nuts
250 mL (1 cup) melted butter
250 mL (1 cup) sugar
5 mL (1 teaspoon) cinnamon
750 mL (3 cups) flour
20 mL (4 teaspoons) baking powder
1 pinch salt
250 mL (1 cup) milk
2 eggs

Method
— Combine the brown sugar, nuts and 50 mL (1/4 cup) melted butter and divide among 12 prepared muffin pans; set aside.
— Combine 125 mL (1/2 cup) sugar, 50 mL (1/4 cup) melted butter and the cinnamon; set aside.
— Sift the flour, baking powder and salt, then add the remaining 125 mL (1/2 cup) of sugar.
— In a bowl, beat the milk, eggs, and remaining melted butter. Using a fork, combine this mixture with the dry ingredients.
— Turn out of the bowl and knead a dozen times, then roll out with a rolling pin to 30 cm x 40 cm (12 in x 16 in).
— Sprinkle the sugar, butter and cinnamon mixture evenly over the dough.
— Roll up the dough lengthwise, pinching the edges to seal.
— Slice into 12 pieces and place in the muffin pans.
— Place the first muffin pan on a raised rack and cook at 90% for 3 to 4 minutes, giving the dish a half-turn halfway through the cooking time.
— Let stand for 2 minutes and turn out.
— Repeat with the second pan.

Sweet Dough

Level of Difficulty	▯▯ ▯▯ ▯▯
Preparation Time	25 min
Cost per Serving	$
Yield	3 dozen brioches
Cooking Time	33 min
Standing Time	None
Power Level	70%, 100%
Write Your Cooking Time Here	

Ingredients
10 mL (2 teaspoons) sugar
250 mL (1 cup) warm water
2 packages active dry yeast
250 mL (1 cup) milk
125 mL (1/2 cup) sugar
50 mL (1/4 cup) butter
5 mL (1 teaspoon) salt
1.5 L (6 cups) whole wheat flour
2 beaten eggs
vegetable oil

Method
— Dissolve 10 mL (2 teaspoons) sugar in warm water; sprinkle with the yeast and set aside for 10 minutes without stirring.
— Heat the milk at 70% for 3 minutes, then add 125 mL (1/2 cup) sugar, butter and salt. Transfer to a large bowl and cool to lukewarm.
— Add the yeast mixture and mix well.
— Add half the flour, beating with a wooden spoon until the mixture becomes elastic.
— Add the eggs and continue to beat, adding enough additional flour to obtain a smooth dough.
— Turn out onto a floured surface and knead until smooth and elastic, about 8 to 10 minutes.
— Shape into 10 balls, brush with a little vegetable oil and set them in a dish. Cover loosely with plastic wrap.
— Half fill another flat dish with warm water.
— Put the dish with the balls of dough into this second dish and let rise at 10% for 25 to 30 minutes or until the dough has doubled in volume.
— Punch down the dough, divide into three parts and freeze, if desired.

Sprinkle the yeast over the sugared water, then set aside for 10 minutes, without stirring.

Knead the dough until smooth and elastic.

Shape the dough into balls, place in a dish and cover loosely with plastic wrap. Put the dish in another dish, half-filled with warm water.

Hot Cross Buns

Level of Difficulty	🍴🍴 🍴🍴 🍴🍴
Preparation Time	25 min
Cost per Serving	**$** **$**
Yield	3 dozen
Cooking Time	20 min
Standing Time	None
Power Level	70%
Write Your Cooking Time Here	

Ingredients
1 sweet dough recipe, page 28
10 mL (2 teaspoons) cinnamon
50 mL (1/4 cup) flour
250 mL (1 cup) raisins
125 mL (1/2 cup) candied fruit
45 mL (3 tablespoons) melted butter
45 mL (3 tablespoons) cinnamon sugar
boiling water
500 mL (2 cups) icing sugar

Method
— Prepare the sweet dough according to the directions on page 28, with the following 3 changes:
1. Add 10 mL (2 teaspoons) cinnamon when stirring in the flour the first time.
2. Put the raisins and candied fruit in a bowl and sprinkle with 50 mL (1/4 cup) flour; toss until coated, then add to the sweet dough when adding flour the second time.
3. Knead the dough as directed for 8 to 10 minutes, then divide into 36 equal parts and shape into smooth balls.
— Place the balls of dough on muffin pans sprayed with an anti-stick agent, such as Pam.
— Combine the melted butter and cinnamon sugar and brush over the buns.
— Cover with a clean towel and set aside in a warm place to rise; when the dough is half risen mark a cross on the top of each bun.
— Put each pan on a raised rack in the oven and cook

at 70% for 4 to 5 minutes, giving the dish a half-turn halfway through the cooking time.

— Repeat with the other pans.

— Make the icing by adding boiling water to the icing sugar, 15 mL (1 tablespoon) at a time, stirring well until the mixture is runny.

— Make icing crosses on the top of each bun; serve immediately.

Combine the raisins and candied fruit, sprinkle with flour and toss to coat.

Separate the dough into 36 equal parts; shape them into smooth balls.

Caramel and Cherry Ring

Level of Difficulty	🍴
Preparation Time	5 min
Cost per Serving	$ $
Yield	6 to 8
Cooking Time	7 min
Standing Time	2 min
Power Level	100%, 70%
Write Your Cooking Time Here	

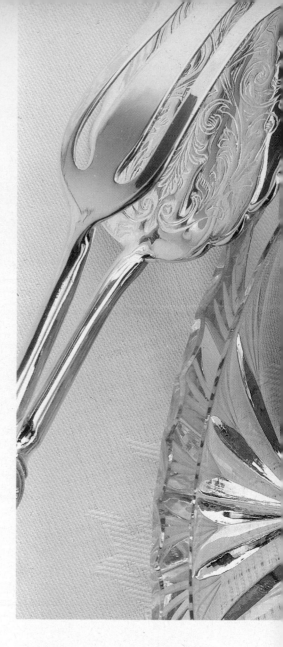

Ingredients
50 mL (1/4 cup) butter
125 mL (1/2 cup) brown sugar, packed
30 mL (2 tablespoons) corn syrup or maple syrup
125 mL (1/2 cup) pecan halves
50 mL (1/4 cup) maraschino cherries, cut in half
1 300 g (10 oz) roll of buttermilk refrigerator rolls

Method
— Put butter in a 20 cm (8 in) tube pan and heat at 100% for 1 minute.
— Sprinkle with brown sugar and add the syrup.
— Stir with a fork and heat at 100% for 45 seconds.
— Sprinkle with the pecans and cherries and arrange the buttermilk rolls in a petal shape on top.
— Cook uncovered at 70% for 4 to 6 minutes.
— Turn out onto a serving platter and let stand for 2 minutes so that the syrup soaks in completely. Serve warm.

MICROTIPS

Cooking Cake Dough Successfully

Cakes are best made in round pans made of glass or in tube pans, which distribute the microwaves evenly. To turn the cake out more easily, cover the bottom of the pan with waxed paper or spray with a non-stick coating. Fill the pan only two-thirds full.

Place the pan on a rack in the oven. If you do not have a special rack, place the pan on an upturned saucer.

Give the cake a half-turn several times during the cooking process to ensure that the microwaves are distributed evenly. Test a cake in a glass pan for doneness by removing it from the oven and inspecting the bottom

visually. The cake is done when a circle 5 cm (2 inches) in diameter remains uncooked at its center. It will finish cooking during the standing time.

Test for doneness in a tube pan by inserting a toothpick in the cake halfway between the center and the sides. If it comes out clean, the cake is done.

Cakes: A Dessert for Celebrations

Cakes are for special occasions, big or small. Indeed, eating a cake is a special occasion in its own right and the universal popularity of cakes has made them kings of the vast realm of desserts. We think immediately of a cake when we want to turn an ordinary supper into a special occasion or a celebration. Since earliest times, cakes have been eaten to celebrate cultural and religious holidays. The development of wheat farming and the flour mill, the importation of new products such as cane sugar — which gradually replaced honey as a sweetener — and the discoveries and international exchanges in the field of culinary art all contributed to making the cake a festive dessert *par excellence*. Engagements, weddings, baptisms, birthdays and holidays such as New Year's Day, Epiphany, Easter, Thanksgiving and Christmas are all traditional occasions on which to share a cake at the end of a beautiful meal.

It is difficult to give a precise definition of a cake since this type of dessert includes a very wide range of recipes. Usually, they are sweet and made with a raised dough or from flaky pastry, short pastry, shortbread, chou pastry, cookies, meringues, etc., which may form the base of the cake. A whole range of diverse ingredients such as creams, icings, fruit garnishes, cheeses, syrups, liqueurs, etc., can then be added.

Because there is such an incredible variety of cakes, it is impossible to imagine anyone not liking them. Some cakes are lightly sweetened while others are made with generous quantities of honey, sugar or brown sugar.

The recipes that follow will give you an extraordinary glimpse into the universe of cakes. Even if the names are familiar, you will continue to make new discoveries. And there is no need to wait for the next celebration to try them.

German Chocolate Cake

Level of Difficulty	🍴
Preparation Time	15 min
Cost per Serving	$ $
Number of Servings	10
Cooking Time	22 min
Standing Time	10 min (per cake layer)
Power Level	50%, 70%, 100%
Write Your Cooking Time Here	

Ingredients

Cake:
4 squares unsweetened chocolate
5 mL (1 teaspoon) oil
175 mL (3/4 cup) butter
375 mL (1-1/2 cups) sugar
3 egg yolks
5 mL (1 teaspoon) vanilla
375 mL (1-1/2 cups) flour
10 mL (2 teaspoons) baking powder
2 mL (1/2 teaspoon) salt
175 to 250 mL (3/4 to 1 cup) milk

Icing:
150 mL (2/3 cup) condensed milk
125 mL (1/2 cup) sugar
2 egg yolks
250 mL (1 cup) grated coconut
250 mL (1 cup) chopped pecans

Method

— Put the chocolate and oil in a bowl and melt at 50% for 4 to 5 minutes, stirring once after 2 minutes; let cool.
— Add the butter, sugar, egg yolks and vanilla to the cooled mixture.
— Sift the flour, baking powder and salt.
— Add the dry ingredients to the butter mixture alternately with the milk, adding only enough milk to make a firm dough.
— Spray two round 22.5 cm (9 in) pans with a non-stick agent such as Pam; or line the pans with waxed paper.
— Divide the batter between the two pans.
— Cook each cake layer separately. Place on a rack in the oven and cook at 70% for 3 minutes.
— Give the dish a half-turn and continue cooking at 70% for 2 to 3 minutes. Test for doneness by inserting a toothpick.
— Let stand for 10 minutes so that the top of the cake dries.
— Repeat with the second cake layer.
— To make the icing,

combine the condensed milk, sugar and egg yolks.
— Cook at 100% for 3 to 4 minutes, or until the mixture thickens, stirring every minute.
— Add the grated coconut and pecans and cook at 100% for 2 minutes, stirring after 1 minute.
— Let the cake cool before icing it.

A winning combination of ingredients: that's the secret of this extraordinary recipe.

MICROTIPS

To Measure Fat Ingredients Easily
Pour 125 mL (1/2 cup) cold water into a measuring cup and drop the butter, lard or shortening by spoonfuls into the cup until the level of the water reaches the desired quantity of the fat ingredient plus 125 mL (1/2 cup).

Peanut Butter Cake

Level of Difficulty	 🍴
Preparation Time	20 min
Cost per Serving	$
Number of Servings	8
Cooking Time	19 min
Standing Time	15 min
Power Level	50%
Write Your Cooking Time Here	

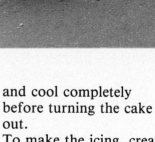

Ingredients

Cake:
125 mL (1/2 cup) butter
300 mL (1-1/4 cups) sugar
50 mL (1/4 cup) peanut butter
2 eggs
5 mL (1 teaspoon) vanilla
500 mL (2 cups) flour
15 mL (1 tablespoon) baking powder
2 mL (1/2 teaspoon) salt
250 mL (1 cup) milk

Icing
50 mL (1/4 cup) butter
50 mL (1/4 cup) peanut butter
5 mL (1 teaspoon) vanilla
50 mL (1/4 cup) milk
625 mL (2-1/2 cups) sifted icing sugar
cherry jam

Method

— Cream the butter, add the sugar and mix well.
— Add the peanut butter; beat in the eggs and vanilla.
— Sift the flour, baking powder and salt.
— Add the dry ingredients to the peanut butter mixture alternately with the milk, beginning and ending with the dry ingredients.
— Butter the inside of a 32.5 cm x 22.5 cm (13 in x 9 in) pan.
— Pour the batter into the pan, spreading it evenly.
— Cook on a rack at 50% for 17 to 19 minutes; cover the ends of the pan with strips of aluminum foil and give the dish a half-turn halfway through the cooking time.

and cool completely before turning the cake out.
— To make the icing, cream the butter, peanut butter and vanilla.
— Add the milk, alternately with the icing sugar, and beat until the mixture becomes light and fluffy.
— Frost the cake and garnish with cherry jam.

MICROTIPS

Cover the ends of the pan with strips of aluminum foil to prevent overcooking.

To Unmold a Frozen Dessert
Unmolding a frozen dessert can be tricky. A simple method is to chill the serving plate, place it over the mold and, holding tightly, invert the mold and its plate. Lift the mold off carefully.

Mandarin Cheesecake

Level of Difficulty	
Preparation Time	15 min
Cost per Serving	**$**
Number of Servings	8
Cooking Time	11 min
Standing Time	30 min
Power Level	100%, 70%
Write Your Cooking Time Here	

Ingredients
50 mL (1/4 cup) melted butter
250 mL (1 cup) chocolate or graham wafer crumbs
1 284 mL (10 oz) can mandarin orange sections
225 g (8 oz) cream cheese
1 beaten egg
75 mL (1/3 cup) sugar
75 mL (1/3 cup) sour cream
1 mint sprig

Method
— Combine the melted butter and wafer crumbs.
— Press into the bottom and sides of a glass plate.
— Cook on a rack at 100% for 1 to 1-1/2 minutes, giving the dish a half-turn once during the cooking time.
— Let cool.
— Reserve 12 mandarin sections and chop the rest.
— In a bowl, beat the cream cheese, egg, sugar and sour cream until smooth, add the chopped mandarin pieces.
— Pour the batter into the crust and place on a rack in the oven; cook at 70% for 6 to 9 minutes or until the center is almost set.
— Let cool and garnish with mandarin sections and the mint sprig before serving.

Boston Cream Cake

Level of Difficulty	🍴🍴
Preparation Time	35 min
Cost per Serving	$
Number of Servings	8
Cooking Time	20 min
Standing Time	7 min
Power Level	100%, 70%
Write Your Cooking Time Here	

Ingredients
Cake:
7 egg whites
325 mL (1-1/3 cups) sugar
7 egg yolks
75 mL (1/3 cup) oil
375 mL (1-1/2 cups) flour
15 mL (1 tablespoon) baking powder
1 pinch salt
5 mL (1 teaspoon) vanilla

Vanilla Cream:
125 mL (1/2 cup) sugar
30 mL (2 tablespoons) cornstarch
15 mL (1 tablespoon) flour
1 mL (1/4 teaspoon) salt
500 mL (2 cups) milk
3 or 4 egg yolks, lightly beaten
30 mL (2 tablespoons) butter
5 mL (1 teaspoon) vanilla

Fudge:
125 mL (1/2 cup) hot water
30 mL (2 tablespoons) honey
105 mL (3-1/2 oz) vegetable fat
30 mL (1 oz) butter
175 mL (3/4 cup) cocoa
1 pinch salt
875 mL (3-1/2 cups) icing sugar

Method: Fudge
— Combine the hot water and honey and bring to a boil at 100% for 60 to 80 seconds.
— Add the vegetable fat and butter and mix well.
— Blend in the cocoa and salt.
— Slowly add the icing sugar until the mixture is firm but still slightly liquid; set aside.

Method: Cake
— Beat the egg whites to stiff peaks and gradually add the sugar.
— Beat the egg yolks and add them gradually to the whites.
— Slowly add the oil, then stir in the flour, baking powder, salt and vanilla.
— Pour the batter into 3 round pans, lined with waxed paper.
— Place one pan on a rack in the oven and cook at 70% for 3 minutes. Give the dish a half-turn and continue cooking at 70%

for 2 minutes or until cooked. Repeat for the other two pans.
— Let stand for 5 to 7 minutes.

Method: Vanilla Cream
— In a mixing bowl, combine the sugar, cornstarch, flour and salt.
— Slowly stir in the milk and cook at 100% until thickened, stirring every 2 minutes.
— Add 1/3 of this mixture to the lightly beaten egg yolks.

— Stir well, then add the remaining milk and combine thoroughly.
— Cook at 100% until thickened, stirring after every minute.
— Stir in the butter and vanilla.
— Let cool at room temperature.
— If thicker cream is desired, increase the flour to 45 mL (3 tablespoons) or add 2 beaten whole eggs.

Preparing the Cake
— Put one layer of cake on a serving platter and cover with half the vanilla cream.
— Cover with another layer of cake and the remaining vanilla cream.
— Top with the last layer and cover with the fudge mixture, so that it runs unevenly over the edges and down the sides.
— Refrigerate.

Tomato Cake

Level of Difficulty	🍴
Preparation Time	15 min
Cost per Serving	$ $
Number of Servings	12
Cooking Time	12 min
Standing Time	15 min
Power Level	70%, 100%
Write Your Cooking Time Here	

Ingredients
425 mL (1-3/4 cups) flour
12 mL (2-1/2 teaspoons) baking powder
2 mL (1/2 teaspoon) baking soda
2 mL (1/2 teaspoon) ground cloves
2 mL (1/2 teaspoon) cinnamon
2 mL (1/2 teaspoon) nutmeg
250 mL (1 cup) raisins
125 mL (1/2 cup) nuts
125 mL (1/2 cup) vegetable fat
250 mL (1 cup) sugar
2 beaten eggs
1 284 mL (10 oz) can tomato paste

Method
— Sift the flour, baking powder, baking soda and spices.
— Combine the raisins and nuts and dust with some of the flour mixture; set aside.
— Beat the vegetable fat and sugar until light and fluffy, then blend in the eggs; beat well and slowly add the dry ingredients alternately with the tomato paste; stir until smooth.
— Add the nuts and raisins.
— Spray the inside of a tube pan with an anti-stick ingredient such as Pam; spoon the batter into the pan.
— Place on a raised rack in the oven and cook at 70% for 10 minutes, giving the pan a half-turn after 5 minutes.
— Increase the power to 100%, give the dish a half-turn, and cook for 1 to 2 minutes.
— Let cool before turning the cake out of the pan.

Assemble the ingredients required to prepare this tomato cake. It is always a popular dessert.

Dust the nuts and raisins with a little of the flour mixture.

Finally, add the nuts and raisins to the batter.

Fruit: A Natural Dessert

Of all the foods in the world, fruits are probably the most treasured. They are flowers that have matured and many fruits have kept much of the flowers' beauty. They are naturally sweet, often smooth and always inviting. It is not surprising that fruits are symbols of temptation in many mythologies! Exotic fruits are even more precious. Until recently, fruits from foreign lands were luxuries and were not widely available. Why, there was a time — not so long ago — when Christmas stockings contained an extraordinary treat; oranges. Fortunately, exotic fruits are now much more accessible. Contrary to popular belief, the diversity and abundance of fruits is due not only to nature's generosity. Nature is, in fact, constantly stimulated by human ingenuity. Many varieties of fruit are the result of patiently applied agrarian practices, which have been perfected over centuries.

Fruits are exciting ingredients to use and they do not necessarily require cooking. A dramatic dessert often requires only a special way of presenting fruit or an interesting new combination of fruits. Their natural flavor does the rest.

Desserts made from uncooked fruits range from colorful salads to elaborate cheese and fruit combinations. Other fruit desserts include fruits bathed in syrup, set in jelly or garnished with sorbets or ice creams.

The variety of desserts made with cooked fruits is inexhaustible. Some recipes are simple, requiring only that the fruits be cooked in a flavored syrup or liqueur; some recipes combine fruits with other ingredients. And of course, there are many recipes for pastries made even more delicious with the addition of a fruit garnish: tarts, pies, puddings, etc.

Fruit desserts are not just an excuse to indulge a sweet tooth. They are the products of many years of culinary experimentation, which makes each combination of ingredients a unique experience.

46

Caramel Apples

Ingredients
8 small apples
juice of 1 lemon
400 g (14 oz) caramel candies
30 mL (2 tablespoons) water
75 mL (1/3 cup) nuts, finely
chopped

Method
— Core the apples and cut
  into quarters.
— Sprinkle with lemon juice
  and set aside.
— Put the caramels and
  water into a bowl and
  cook at 70% for 2
  minutes.
— Stir in the nuts; cook for
  another 1 to 2 minutes,
  stirring once during the
  cooking time.
— Pierce each piece of apple
  with a fork and dip in the
  melted cramel.
— Shake to remove the
  excess candy.
— Put the apple quarters on
  a piece of greased waxed
  paper.
— Let set and cool.

Level of Difficulty	🍴
Preparation Time	10 min
Cost per Serving	$
Number of Servings	8
Cooking Time	4 min
Standing Time	10 min
Power Level	70%
Write Your Cooking Time Here	

Applesauce Cookies

Ingredients
250 mL (1/2 cup) applesauce
150 mL (2/3 cup) raisins
125 mL (1/2 cup) candied
fruits, chopped
400 mL (1-2/3 cups) flour
2 mL (1/2 teaspoon) baking
soda
5 mL (1 teaspoon) baking
powder
2 mL (1/2 teaspoon) salt
5 mL (1 teaspoon) nutmeg
5 mL (1 teaspoon) cinnamon
250 mL (1 cup) butter
400 mL (1-2/3 cups) brown
sugar
125 mL (1/2 cup) coffee
250 mL (1 cup) applesauce

Method
— Dust the raisins and fruits
  with a little of the flour;
  set aside.
— Sift the remaining flour,
  baking soda, baking
  powder, salt, nutmeg and
  cinnamon; set aside.
— Cream the butter and
  brown sugar
— Stir in the coffee and
  applesauce, then add the
  dry ingredients and
  raisins.

— Combine thoroughly.
— Drop spoonfuls of dough
  on a greased, microwave-
  safe cookie sheet.
— Place on a rack in the
  oven and cook at 70% for
  4 minutes, giving the dish
  a half-turn after 2
  minutes.
— Remove the cookies, place
  on a rack and let cool.
— Repeat with the remaining
  dough.

Apple and Coconut Brown Betty

Level of Difficulty	🍴
Preparation Time	10 min
Cost per Serving	$
Number of Servings	6
Cooking Time	5 min
Standing Time	2 min
Power Level	100%
Write Your Cooking Time Here	

Ingredients
8 apples, cored, peeled and sliced
250 mL (1 cup) oatmeal
250 mL (1 cup) grated coconut
250 mL (1 cup) brown sugar
75 mL (1/3 cup) butter
250 mL (1 cup) walnuts, chopped coarsely

Method
— Combine the oatmeal, coconut, brown sugar and butter; set aside.
— Arrange half the apple slices in a single layer in a baking dish; cover with half the oatmeal and mixture.
— Arrange the remaining apple slices on top; cover with the remaining oatmeal mixture.
— Sprinkle with walnuts, and cook at 100% for 4 to 5 minutes, giving the dish a half-turn halfway through the cooking time.
— Let stand for 2 minutes.

Oatmeal, coconut, brown sugar and butter: these are the ingredients required to prepare this apple-based recipe.

Alternate layers of apple slices and the oatmeal and coconut mixture.

Sprinkle with coarsely chopped walnuts before cooking.

MICROTIPS

Watch Out for Sugar
If the dough or batter you are using contains sugar, it is important not to exceed the cooking time indicated in the recipe. Sugar heats rapidly and will burn if overcooked.

Pears in Red Wine

Ingredients
4 pears
250 mL (1 cup) red wine
50 mL (1/4 cup) sugar
zest of one orange, grated
2.5 cm (1 in) cinnamon stick
2 mL (1/2 teaspoon) nutmeg

Method
— Peel the pears, cut them in half lengthwise and remove the cores; set aside.
— Place the remaining ingredients in a dish and heat at 100% for 2 to 3 minutes.
— Carefully set the pear halves in the dish, cut side down.
— Cook at 100% for 3 to 4 minutes, giving the dish a half-turn halfway through the cooking time.
— Remove the pears and set aside.
— Boil the syrup, uncovered at 100% for 10 minutes.
— Let cool completely.
— Pour the cold syrup over the pears before serving.

Level of Difficulty	🍴
Preparation Time	10 min
Cost per Serving	$ $
Number of Servings	4
Cooking Time	17 min
Standing Time	None
Power Level	100%
Write Your Cooking Time Here	

Pears Alma

Ingredients
6 pears
125 mL (1/2 cup) port
250 mL (1 cup) 35% cream
75 mL (1/3 cup) fruit sugar
dark chocolate, grated

Method
— Peel the pears, cut them in half lengthwise and remove cores.
— Set the halves in a dish, cut side down; add the port, cover and cook at 100% for 3 to 4 minutes, or until the pears are tender.
— Remove the pears and let cool.
— Whip the cream, gradually adding the fruit sugar.
— To serve, set pears and syrup in individual fruit bowls. Garnish with whipped cream and sprinkle with grated chocolate.

Level of Difficulty	🍴
Preparation Time	10 min
Cost per Serving	$ $
Number of Servings	6
Cooking Time	4 min
Standing Time	None
Power Level	100%
Write Your Cooking Time Here	

Pears with Maple Syrup

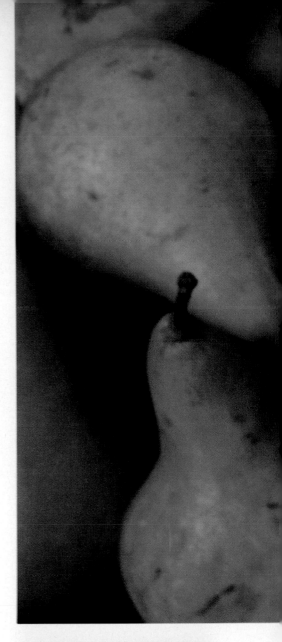

Level of Difficulty	🍴
Preparation Time	5 min
Cost per Serving	**$**
Number of Servings	6
Cooking Time	4 min
Standing Time	2 min
Power Level	100%
Write Your Cooking Time Here	✏️

Ingredients
1 796 mL (28 oz) can of pears
30 mL (2 tablespoons) butter
125 mL (1/2 cup) maple syrup
vanilla ice cream

Method
— Set the pears in a dish.
— Combine the butter and maple syrup and pour over the pears.
— Cover and cook at 100% for 3 to 4 minutes, giving the dish a half-turn halfway through the cooking time.
— Let stand for 2 minutes and put the pears into individual fruit bowls.
— Cover with ice cream and top with the maple syrup mixture.

Pears, butter, maple syrup and ice cream are the only ingredients required for this recipe.

54

Pour the butter and maple syrup mixture over the pears.

Cover and cook at 100% for 3 to 4 minutes, giving the dish a half-turn halfway through the cooking time.

MICROTIPS

Protecting the Flavor of Certain Fruits
The flavor of certain fruits, particularly those with a high acid content, will alter when in contact with metal. When forcing a fruit purée or syrup through a sieve, choose one with a nylon, rather than a metal basket.

Pineapple Flan

Ingredients
8 slices pineapple
7 strawberries
500 mL (2 cups) milk
1 mL (1/4 teaspoon) salt
5 mL (1 teaspoon) vanilla
75 mL (1/3 cup) cornstarch
175 mL (3/4 cup) sugar
2 large eggs, beaten
1 pie crust, 22.5 cm (9 in)
diameter

Method
— Combine the milk, salt
and vanilla and heat at
100% for 4 to 5 minutes,
until the liquid is warm,
stirring every 2 minutes;
set aside.
— In a bowl, combine the
cornstarch and sugar, then
add the beaten eggs. Stir
in the warm milk.
— Cook at 100% for 3 to 4
minutes, stirring every
minute.
— Finely chop one pineapple
slice and add it to the
filling.
— Pour into the crust and
garnish with the pineapple
slices and strawberries.

Level of Difficulty	🍴
Preparation Time	15 min
Cost per Serving	$
Number of Servings	8
Cooking Time	9 min
Standing Time	None
Power Level	100%
Write Your Cooking Time Here	

Fruit Gratin

Ingredients
1 banana, coarsely chopped
500 mL (2 cups) applesauce
500 mL (2 cups) frozen
unsweetened raspberries
15 mL (1 tablespoon) orange
marmalade
125 mL (1/2 cup) granola,
such as Harvest Crunch

Method
— Combine the fruits,
applesauce and marmalade
in a dish.
— Cover with the granola
and cook at 100% for 3
to 4 minutes, giving the
dish a half-turn halfway
through the cooking time.
— Let stand for 2 minutes
before serving.

Level of Difficulty	🍴
Preparation Time	5 min
Cost per Serving	$
Number of Servings	6
Cooking Time	4 min
Standing Time	2 min
Power Level	100%
Write Your Cooking Time Here	

Pineapple Fruit Salad

Level of Difficulty	🍴🍴
Preparation Time	20 min
Cost per Serving	$ $
Number of Servings	6
Cooking Time	1 min
Standing Time	None
Power Level	100%
Write Your Cooking Time Here	

Ingredients
1 whole pineapple
1 284 mL (10 oz) can mandarin sections
125 mL (1/2 cup) candied cherries
125 mL (1/2 cup) roasted almonds
125 mL (1/2 cup) orange marmalade
50 mL (1/4 cup) rum

Method
— Put the pineapple on a flat surface and cut it in half lengthwise, without removing the leaves.
— Remove the tough centre, scoop out the flesh and cut into pieces. Set the shells aside.
— In a bowl, combine the pineapple pieces, mandarin sections, candied cherries and almonds; set aside.
— Heat the marmalade at 100% for 30 seconds. Pour over the fruit.
— Arrange the pineaple shells on a platter and fill with the fruit mixture.
— Heat the rum at 100% for 15 to 20 seconds, then ignite.
— Pour the flambéed rum over the pineapples and serve.

MICROTIPS

Softening Refrigerated Butter
Put 100 g butter into the microwave and heat at 10% for 30 seconds, giving the dish a half-turn after 5 seconds. Do not overcook as the butter will melt.

Stale Bread for Puddings
Stale bread is an ingredient in several pudding recipes. Do not replace this ingredient with fresh bread because it will not absorb sufficient liquid. If you have no stale bread, put 1 slice of fresh bread into the microwave oven on paper towel and cook at 100% for about 1 minute. Let cool completely before using.

Molded Cream with Fruit Sauce

Level of Difficulty	🍴
Preparation Time	5 min
Cost per Serving	$
Number of Servings	4
Cooking Time	16 min
Standing Time	None
Power Level	100%, 70%
Write Your Cooking Time Here	

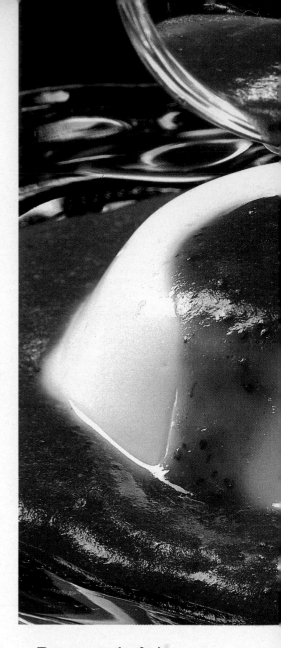

Ingredients
3 eggs
500 mL (2 cups) milk
15 mL (1 tablespoon) brown sugar
5 mL (1 teaspoon) vanilla

Fruit Sauce:
500 mL (2 cups) strawberries
15 mL (1 tablespoon) brown sugar
juice of 1 lemon

Method
— Beat the eggs with a whisk.
— In a bowl, combine the milk and brown sugar, and heat at 100% for 2 minutes.
— Add the beaten eggs and vanilla to the warm milk mixture.
— Pour the mixture into 4 ramekins.
— Place the ramekins on a rack in the oven and cook at 70% for 7 minutes.
— Give each of the ramekins a half-turn and continue cooking at 70% for 6 to 7 minutes, or until the mixture is cooked. Let cool.
— To prepare the fruit sauce, place the ingredients in a blender and purée.
— Divide the sauce evenly among four dessert plates. Invert a ramekin in the center of each plate.

Make sure the ingredients are very fresh so that this recipe will have a delicate flavor.

Pour equal amounts of the custard mixture into the four ramekins.

MICROTIPS

To Improve a Too Sweet Dessert
The sweet taste of certain fruit desserts can be reduced by garnishing them with equal parts of Chantilly cream and sour cream or yogurt, topped with chopped nuts.

Mandarin and Ginger Sorbet

Level of Difficulty	🍴🍴
Preparation Time	10 min
Cost per Serving	$
Number of Servings	6
Cooking Time	7 min
Standing Time	None
Power Level	100%
Write Your Cooking Time Here	✏️🍎

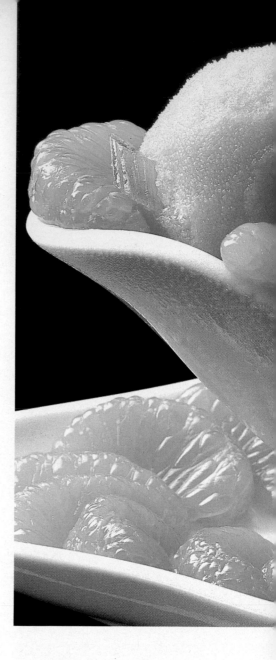

Ingredients
2 284 mL (10 oz) cans
mandarin sections
30 mL (2 tablespoons)
candied ginger, in pieces
50 mL (1/4 cup) sugar
15 mL (1 tablespoon)
cornstarch
125 mL (1/2 cup) orange
juice
30 mL (2 tablespoons) rum

Method
— Drain the mandarin
  sections and set aside;
  reserve the juice.
— In a bowl, combine the
  juice, ginger and sugar;
  heat at 100% for 2 to 3
  minutes, or until the
  liquid reaches the boiling
  point.
— Combine the cornstarch
  and orange juice and add
  to the hot mixture.
— Cook at 100% for 3 to 4
  minutes, stirring halfway
  through the cooking time.
— Add the mandarin
  sections and the rum, and
  pour into a large dish to
  cool quickly to room
  temperature.
— Purée in a blender or food
  processor.
— Pour into a metal cake
  pan and freeze for 3 to 4
  hours, stirring every 30
  minutes, until firm or
  freeze in a ice-cream
  maker according to the
  manufacturer's
  instructions.

Assemble the ingredients for this pleasing dessert.

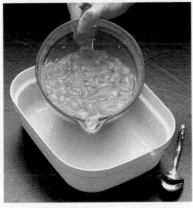

After adding the rum and the madarin sections, pour into a large dish to cool to room temperature.

MICROTIPS

To Turn Out a Cake
When cooking a cake in a glass dish, you can cover the inside of the dish with plastic wrap instead of lining it with waxed paper. This makes the cake easier to turn out and the dish easier to clean.

A Panorama of Puddings

Puddings are an unusual type of dessert and the term itself is all the more unusual because so many different types of foods are grouped under the same label. Indeed what does a Yorkshire Pudding — a milk and egg batter cooked in roast beef drippings — have in common with a starchy, sweet and creamy mixture served in individual cups?

Clearly not very much. So here we will limit ourselves to describing dessert puddings and we will take a look at two or three different types.

The original pudding is English. It was a sweet dessert, served hot or cold, prepared with either a pastry, breadcrumb or cookie base or with a rice or semolina base. The batter often contained fruits, fresh, dried or candied, and sometimes spiced. The pudding was then covered with a sweet sauce (often prepared with fruit) or with an English cream.

The best known English puddings are Christmas Pudding and Plum Pudding. Both are cooked in boiling water and must stand for some time before being reheated or flambéed. They may be served with jam or a rum cream.

Outside Great Britain there are many other puddings which have also become classics. Rice, tapioca, semolina and bread puddings have all acquired solid reputations. Gourmet cooking includes a small repertory of puddings of which the Diplomat is the best known in North America, the term pudding includes a variety of starchy mixtures flavored with sweet ingredients such as caramel or chocolate. These desserts do not contain cereal, semolina or pastry and so do not conform to the strict definition of pudding.

The word pudding may also refer to a cake made of left-over desserts (pieces of cake or brioche), milk, sugar, raisins and eggs. This type of pudding is often flavored with rum and candied orange peel and is served chilled.

Now that the whole family of puddings is a little more familiar to you, it's up to you to discover all the delicious recipes described in the following pages.

Rice Pudding

Level of Difficulty	🍴
Preparation Time	5 min
Cost per Serving	$
Number of Servings	approximately 6
Cooking Time	25 min
Standing Time	None
Power Level	100%, 70%
Write Your Cooking Time Here	

Ingredients
250 mL (1 cup) long grain rice, uncooked
500 mL (2 cups) hot water
125 mL (1/2 cup) sugar
30 mL (2 tablespoons) cornstarch
1 mL (1/4 teaspoon) salt
625 mL (2-1/2 cups) milk
2 egg yolks, beaten
2 mL (1/2 teaspoon) vanilla
125 mL (1/2 cup) raisins
nutmeg

Method
— Pour the rice and hot water into a dish; cover and cook at 100% for 5 minutes.
— Reduce the power to 70% and continue cooking for 10 minutes; set aside.
— In a bowl, combine the sugar, cornstarch and salt; gradually add the milk and egg yolks.
— Stir in the cooked rice, vanilla and raisins.
— Cook at 100% for 8 to 10 minutes, stirring every 2 minutes.
— Pour into individual cups and sprinkle with nutmeg before serving.

Healthy, nourishing, simple ingredients are the basis of this memorable dessert.

66

MICROTIPS

Do Not Overbeat Cake Batter
The ingredients which make up a cake batter are in a fragile chemical balance. For this reason, avoid overbeating the batter as this prevents the cake from rising.

To Maximize the Volume of Egg Whites
Egg whites that have been kept in the refrigerator cannot be beaten to the same volume as egg whites at room temperature. You can get around this by heating the egg whites in the microwave at 100% for 5 seconds. Do not heat for any longer or they will toughen.

Cooking with Sugar
If your mixture contains a lot of sugar, take care not to cook it for longer than the recipe directs. Sugar can get too hot very quickly, at which point it may burn.

Tapioca Pudding

Ingredients
500 mL (2 cups) milk
2 eggs
75 mL (1/3 cup) sugar
50 mL (1/4 cup) quick
cooking tapioca
5 mL (1 teaspoon) vanilla
pinch salt
2 mL (1/2 teaspoon) nutmeg

Method
— In a bowl, combine all the
  ingredients.
— Cook at 100% for 7 to 8
  minutes or until the
  mixture thickens, stirring
  every 2 minutes.
— Pour into 6 small dessert
  bowls and let cool before
  serving.

Level of Difficulty	
Preparation Time	5 min
Cost per Serving	$
Number of Servings	6
Cooking Time	8 min
Standing Time	None
Power Level	100%
Write Your Cooking Time Here	

Black Magic Pudding

Ingredients
250 mL (1 cup) flour
375 mL (1-1/2 cup) sugar
10 mL (2 teaspoons) baking
powder
1 mL (1/4 teaspoon) salt
125 mL (1/2 cup) melted
butter
125 mL (1/2 cup) cocoa
125 mL (1/2 cup) milk
5 mL (1 teaspoon) vanilla
125 mL (1/2 cup) chopped
nuts
175 mL (3/4 cup) boiling
water

Method
— Combine the flour, half
 the sugar, baking powder
 and salt; set aside.
— Mix the melted butter
 with half the cocoa; set
 aside.
— Combine the milk and
 vanilla; set aside.
— Beat the three mixtures
 together and pour into a
 20 cm (8 in) square pan.
— Combine the remaining
 sugar and cocoa and add
 the nuts; sprinkle over the
 top of the cake.
— Carefully pour boiling

water on top; do not mix.
— Cover the 4 edges of the
 pan with strips of
 aluminum foil and cook
 on a raised rack at 50%
 for 22 to 26 minutes,
 giving the dish a half-turn
 halfway through the
 cooking time.
— After 16 minutes check
 for doneness at the 4
 corners of the pan;
 remove the aluminum foil
 strips if this part is
 cooking too slowly.
— Let stand for 10 minutes
 and serve warm.

Bread Pudding

Ingredients
8 or 10 slices of bread
125 mL (1/2 cup) raisins
3 eggs
125 mL (1/2 cup) brown
sugar, packed
5 mL (1 teaspoon) vanilla
salt
500 mL (2 cups) milk
30 mL (2 tablespoons) butter
cinnamon

Method
— Cut the bread slices into
cubes. There should be 1
L (4 cups). Add the
raisins; set aside.
— Beat the eggs; add the
brown sugar, vanilla and
salt; stir until smooth; set
aside.
— In a bowl, place the milk
and butter; heat at 100%
for 4 to 5 minutes.
— Gradually stir the beaten
egg mixture into the hot
milk.
— Pour over the bread cubes
and raisins; sprinkle with
cinnamon.
— Cook at 50% for 8 to 10
minutes, or until the
mixture is cooked, giving
the dish a half-turn
halfway through the
cooking time.
— Let stand for 4 minutes to
complete cooking.

Lemon and Pineapple Pudding

Ingredients
175 mL (3/4 cup) sugar
45 mL (3 tablespoons) cornstarch
250 mL (1 cup) crushed pineapple with its juice
150 mL (2/3 cup) water
2 egg yolks
zest from 1 lemon, grated
90 g (3 oz) cream cheese
2 egg whites

Method
— In a bowl, mix 125 mL (1/2 cup) sugar, cornstarch, pineapple with its juice and water.
— Cook at 100% for 3 to 4 minutes, or until the mixture reaches the boiling point, stirring every minute; set aside.
— Beat the egg yolks and add to the pineapple mixture.
— Add the lemon zest and cream cheese and reheat at 70% for 1 minute.
— Beat well until the cream cheese is thoroughly incorporated, then let cool.
— Beat the egg whites to stiff peaks; add the remaining 50 mL (1/4 cup) sugar.
— Carefully fold the egg whites into the pineapple mixture.
— Pour into individual dessert bowls.

Apple Crumble

Level of Difficulty	
Preparation Time	20 min
Cost per Serving	$
Number of Servings	10
Cooking Time	24 min
Standing Time	None
Power Level	50%
Write Your Cooking Time Here	

Ingredients
8 slices stale bread
60 mL (4 tablespoons) melted butter
500 mL (2 cups) applesauce
10 mL (2 teaspoons) nutmeg
125 mL (1/2 cup) raisins
2 beaten eggs
375 mL (1-1/2 cups) milk
50 mL (1/4 cup) sugar
5 mL (1 teaspoon) vanilla
75 mL (1/3 cup) brown sugar
cream

Method
— Spray a 22.5 cm x 16.25 cm (9 in x 6.5 in) soufflé dish with an anti-stick agent such as Pam.
— Remove the crusts from the bread; brush the bread with the melted butter and cut each slice into 4 squares.
— Line the dish with one third of the bread, then add half the applesauce.
— Sprinkle with half the nutmeg and half the raisins.
— Add one third more bread, then the remaining applesauce, nutmeg and raisins.
— Cover with the remaining bread squares; set aside.
— In a bowl, combine the beaten eggs, milk, sugar and vanilla.
— Carefully pour the mixture into the dish and sprinkle with the brown sugar.
— Cook at 50% for 10 minutes and give the dish a half-turn.
— Continue cooking at 50% for 12 to 14 minutes.
— Serve hot, with cream.

Eight slices of bread and these common ingredients combine to make a delicious apple crumble.

Spray the inside of the soufflé dish with a non-stick coating.

Pour half the applesauce over the bottom layer of bread that has been brushed with melted butter. Sprinkle with raisins and nutmeg.

73

Rum Babas

Level of Difficulty	
Preparation Time	20 min
Cost per Serving	$ $
Number of Servings	8
Cooking Time	41 min
Standing Time	10 min
Power Level	100%, 10%, 70%
Write Your Cooking Time Here	

Ingredients

75 mL (1/3 cup) milk
1 package active dry yeast
300 mL (1-1/4 cups) flour
3 eggs, lightly beaten
50 mL (1/4 cup) melted butter
10 mL (2 teaspoons) sugar
2 mL (1/2 teaspoon) salt
75 mL (1/3 cup) raisins
oil
250 mL (1 cup) brown sugar
375 mL (1-1/2 cups) water
175 mL (3/4 cup) rum

Method

— Heat the milk at 100% for 30 seconds or until lukewarm; sprinkle the yeast over the milk and let stand for 10 minutes then stir. Set aside.
— Pour the flour into a bowl and form a well in the centre; pour in the milk mixture and the lightly beaten eggs.
— Beat with a wooden spoon until the dough is smooth.
— Add the melted butter, sugar, salt and raisins; beat well.
— Divide into 8 parts and shape into small balls.
— Grease 8 molds and put a ball of dough in each.
— Brush the top of each ball

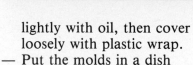

lightly with oil, then cover loosely with plastic wrap.
— Put the molds in a dish containing some warm water.
— Heat at 10% for 25 to 30 minutes or until the dough has doubled in size, changing the position of the molds after the first 15

minutes.
— Remove the dish with the water, uncover the molds and put them on a raised rack.
— Cook at 70% for 2 to 3 minutes or until done; set aside.
— Combine the brown sugar and water and cook at

100% for 6 to 7 minutes, or until boiling; add the rum.
— Turn out the babas onto a serving platter.
— Spoon the sauce over the babas until it is all absorbed.
— Cover and refrigerate before serving.

These are ingredients for Rum Babas, a dessert that is always appreciated.

Mousse:
A Cloud-like Dessert

The term mousse doesn't mean the same thing to everyone. This is not really surprising since culinary tradition varies so much from region to region and not everyone agrees on what should be called mousse and what should be called something else.

Let's agree on the broadest meaning possible and take a look at many different recipes for mousse.

Basically, the main ingredient in a mousse is either beaten eggs or gelatin. Its consistency can vary from creamy to very firm, but it must always be light. Its ingredients are well blended together or whipped.

A mousse can be flavored with fruits, herbs, chocolate, caramel, etc. Many mousse recipes are flavored and enriched with the addition of alcohol. One famous recipe for mousse is flavored with red wine. Most mousses are served cold, but some may be served warm and others, like the celebrated zabaglione, are brought to the table hot.

Creams are some of the easiest desserts to prepare. They are made with milk, eggs, sugar and butter, and sometimes are thickened with flour. Creams can be flavored in many ways.

Some recipes for chocolate mousse and coffee mousse feature stiffly beaten egg whites. Both of these mousses are enlivened with orange, rum or cognac flavoring. Sometimes the coffee and chocolate flavors are combined. Gelatin-based mousses are ideal for setting in molds. They can be made in many different shapes and when combined with colorful fruit, make a very impressive presentation.

At some point, you may want to make a very elaborate mousse to serve to guests, but for now, the recipes that follow are simple and will give you a taste of the light world of mousses.

Chocolate Mint Mousse

Level of Difficulty	(icon)
Preparation Time	10 min
Cost per Serving	$
Number of Servings	8
Cooking Time	6 min
Standing Time	None
Power Level	100%
Write Your Cooking Time Here	(icon)

Ingredients
175 mL (3/4 cup) water
2 squares unsweetened chocolate
200 g (7 oz) chocolate covered mint thins
1 package unflavored gelatin
125 mL (1/2 cup) cold water
250 mL (1 cup) 35% cream

Method
— Heat the water at 100% for 2 minutes.
— Add the chocolate squares and mint thins, and heat at 100% for 3 to 4 minutes, or until the chocolate is melted; set aside.
— Sprinkle gelatin over the cold water; set aside for 5 minutes and then stir until completely dissolved.
— Combine the two mixtures and refrigerate.
— When the mousse begins to set, add the cream and whip vigorously.
— Pour into cups and freeze.

Cherry Mousse

Level of Difficulty	 (icons)
Preparation Time	15 min
Cost per Serving	$ $
Number of Servings	6
Cooking Time	1 min 30 sec
Standing Time	None
Power Level	70%
Write Your Cooking Time Here	

Ingredients
4 egg yolks
125 mL (1/2 cup) milk
50 mL (1/4 cup) cherry syrup
1 pinch salt
1 package unflavored gelatin
125 mL (1/2 cup) maraschino cherries, drained, coarsely chopped
50 mL (1/4 cup) orange juice
15 mL (1 tablespoon) lemon juice
1 mL (1/4 teaspoon) almond essence
4 egg whites
50 mL (1/4 cup) sugar

Method
— Combine the egg yolks, cherry syrup and salt; mix well.
— Sprinkle the gelatin over the egg mixture and stir, then heat at 70% for 1 to 1-1/2 minutes or until the gelatin is completely dissolved.
— Let cool.
— Add the cherries, orange juice, lemon juice and almond essence; mix.
— Refrigerate until the mixture has the consistency of an unbeaten egg white.
— Beat the egg whites until stiff, while gradually adding sugar.
— Fold the egg whites into the cherry mixture, then pour into dessert bowls.
— Chill until set.

Beat the egg whites to stiff peaks while gradually adding the sugar.

MICROTIPS

Making the Best Mousse

Some fresh fruits, such as pineapple, contains enzymes which prevent gelatin from setting. In this case, the fruits should be cooked before using (cooking destroys the enzymes) or the fresh fruit should be replaced by fruit jam.

Some alcoholic products add a delicious flavor to mousses. Madeira, for example, adds character to an apricot mousse and coffee liqueur will enhance a mocha mousse. Sweet white wine, kirsch, maraschino liqueur and even champagne are all delicious ingredients.

Grape Mousse

Level of Difficulty	
Preparation Time	10 min
Cost per Serving	$
Number of Servings	6
Cooking Time	1 min
Standing Time	None
Power Level	100%
Write Your Cooking Time Here	

Ingredients
1-1/2 packages unflavored gelatin
375 mL (1-1/2 cups) carbonated grape juice
45 mL (3 tablespoons) lemon juice
125 mL (1/2 cup) condensed milk, frozen
15 mL (1 tablespoon) sugar
225 g (8 oz) unsweetened pineapple slices

Method
— Sprinkle the gelatin onto 50 mL (1/4 cup) of the carbonated grape juice and let dissolve for 1 to 2 minutes.
— Heat at 100% for 1 minute.
— Add the remaining grape juice and 30 mL (2 tablespoons) lemon juice; refrigerate the mixture until half set.
— In a bowl, beat the condensed milk until thickened, then add the remaining lemon juice and sugar, beating until the mixture is firm.
— Combine with the grape mixture.
— Pour into individual sorbet glasses or a lightly oiled mold and chill.
— Unmold and garnish with slices of pineapple before serving.

This dessert is exquisite. First assemble the required ingredients.

Let the gelatin dissolve for 1 to 2 minutes in the carbonated grape juice.

Combine the mixture of condensed milk, lemon juice and sugar with the grape juice jelly.

Crème Caramel

Level of Difficulty	🍴🍴🍴
Preparation Time	15 min
Cost per Serving	$
Number of Servings	4
Cooking Time	21 min
Standing Time	None
Power Level	100%, 50%
Write Your Cooking Time Here	

Ingredients
250 mL (1 cup) sugar
50 mL (1/4 cup) water
500 mL (2 cups) milk
15 mL (1 tablespoon) vanilla
3 whole eggs
2 egg yolks

Method
— Pour half the sugar and 45 mL (3 tablespoons) of water into a bowl.
— Cook at 100% until the mixture is golden, checking for doneness several times.
— Remove the bowl and plunge it immediately into a basin of cold water to stop the cooking process.
— Add the remaining water and heat at 100% for 30 seconds; stir well so that the caramel is combined with the water.
— Pour the mixture into 4 small ramekins; set aside.
— Combine the milk, vanilla and remaining sugar; heat at 100% for 3 to 4 minutes, or until the milk is hot but not boiling.
— In a bowl, beat the whole eggs and the yolks, then gradually add the hot milk mixture.

— Pour into the ramekins.
— Cook uncovered at 50%
  for 10 to 12 minutes,
  giving each ramekin a
  half-turn halfway through
  the cooking time.

Sugar, water, milk, vanilla and eggs are all that is needed to prepare a delicious crème caramel.

To stop the cooking process of the sugar and water immediately, plunge the container into cold water.

The Classic Compote

The word compote makes you think of a cool autumn wind with rain beating against the windows and a steaming bowl of hot apple compote on the table. This memory is a familiar one to many people since apple compote has always been a favorite homemade dessert. Compotes need not be made with apples: almost any kind of fruit can be used. Many can be used alone and most can be mixed with other fruits so that the possible combinations are practically limitless. Here is a list of some fruits which are delicious in a compote: apricots, blueberries, blackcurrants, pineapples, bananas, cherries, quince, figs, strawberries, raspberries, gooseberries, kiwi, mandarins, mangoes, blackberries, melons, oranges, grapefruit, papaya, peach, pears, prunes, grapes, rhubarb, etc. The list is impressive, isn't it?

And what exactly is a compote? The term always refers to fruits, fresh or dried, which have been cooked, whole or in pieces, usually in a clear syrup. The fresh fruits are simply poached, while the dried fruits are first soaked in water that is sometimes flavored with alcohol, tea, etc.

The compote is not puréed; it contains pieces of fruit and so these fruits should be cooked only until they are soft. To add flavor to the juice, it can be boiled with lemon or orange zest, cloves, sticks of cinnamon, vanilla, etc. This will produce a delicious syrup which should then be strained through a sieve and poured over the compote before serving.

The fruits themselves can also be flavored with vanilla, lemon or orange zest, powdered cinnamon, grated coconut, finely chopped almonds, candied fruits, raisins, etc. The range and diversity of compotes make them one of the most celebrated desserts.

Apple Compote

Level of Difficulty	
Preparation Time	15 min
Cost per Serving	$
Number of Servings	3 cups
Cooking Time	12 min
Standing Time	None
Power Level	100%
Write Your Cooking Time Here	

Ingredients
10 to 12 apples
15 mL (1 tablespoon) lemon juice
50 mL (1/4 cup) sugar
cinnamon, to taste

Method
— Peel and core the apples.
— Cut the apples into equal-sized pieces and place in a dish, filling it only half full.
— Sprinkle with lemon juice, sugar and cinnamon.
— Cover and cook at 100% for 10 to 12 minutes, stirring the ingredients every 4 minutes.

It is always a good idea to have some apple compote on hand. First assemble these ingredients.

Place the apple pieces in a dish, filling it only half full.

Stir every 4 minutes during the cooking time, so that the apple pieces cook evenly.

MICROTIPS

Grating Chocolate Easily

Chocolate, when grated to decorate desserts, tends to stick to the grater and to melt when handled. Avoid this problem by refrigerating the chocolate and the grater before using.

Fruit Compote

Level of Difficulty	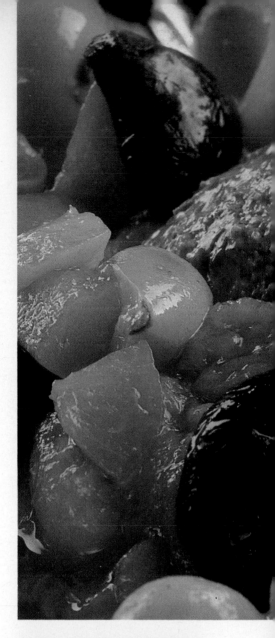
Preparation Time	10 min
Cost per Serving	**$**
Number of Servings	4
Cooking Time	10 min
Standing Time	None
Power Level	100%
Write Your Cooking Time Here	

Ingredients
2 peaches
2 apricots
4 prunes
10 cherries
1 small bunch of seedless grapes

Method
— Remove the stones from the fruits and cut them into pieces.
— Combine them in a dish, filling it half full.
— Cover and cook at 100% for 8 to 10 minutes, stirring 3 times during cooking time.

The harmonious balance of these fresh fruits will give you an exquisite compote in just 20 minutes.

MICROTIPS

**Don't Let the Compote
Become a Purée**
When preparing a
compote of fruits having
different consistencies,
the mixture may become
too soft or the result
may be a mixture of
overcooked and
undercooked fruits. This
can be prevented by
checking the consistency
of the fruits to be used
and by adding the fruits
to the mixture in the
correct order.

You should begin with
large hard fruits such as
apples, pears and
peaches. To accelerate
their cooking time, cut
them in half or in
quarters. Pieces of
pineapple and rhubarb
can also be added at this
time.

Interrupt the cooking
process to add medium
consistency fruits:
oranges, cherries,
bananas and grapes.

Just before the end of
the cooking process add
very fragile fruits such
as melon, blackberries
and raspberries. By
following this method
and with a little
experience, you will
have a perfect compote
full of beautiful pieces
of fruit which will all
melt in your mouth.

Rhubarb Compote

Level of Difficulty	🍴
Preparation Time	15 min
Cost per Serving	$
Number of Servings	4
Cooking Time	10 min
Standing Time	None
Power Level	100%
Write Your Cooking Time Here	

Ingredients
500 mL (2 cups) rhubarb, peeled, cut into 2.5 cm (1 in) pieces
175 mL (3/4 cup) sugar
5 mL (1 teaspoon) grated orange zest
30 mL (2 tablespoons) water

Method
— Combine the ingredients in a dish.
— Cover and cook at 100% for 8 to 10 minutes, stirring every 3 minutes. Serve hot, warm or cold.

During the rhubarb season, nothing can top a rhubarb compote for a quick, delicious dessert.

Peel the rhubarb and cut into 2.5 cm (1 in) pieces.

Stir every 3 minutes during cooking time.

MICROTIPS

Cooking Different Fruits Together

When cooking fruits of different densities together, put the fruits into a round dish, placing the denser fruits (such as apples) close to the edge and the faster cooking fruits (such as strawberries) toward the center of the dish.

Strawberry Jam

Ingredients
3 L (12 cups) strawberries
1.5 L (6 cups) sugar
50 mL (1/4 cup) lemon juice

Method
— Combine the ingredients and let stand for 1 hour.
— Cook in a very large dish (it should be no more than two-third full) at 100% for 40 minutes, then stir.
— Stir and reduce the power to 50% and continue cooking for 30 minutes, stirring twice during the cooking time.
— Stir once more and set aside to cool.
— Pour into sterilized jars and seal.

Level of Difficulty	
Preparation Time	5 min*
Cost per Serving	$
Quantity	approx. 6 cups
Cooking Time	1 h 10 min
Standing Time	None
Power Level	100%, 50%
Write Your Cooking Time Here	

*Marinate the fruit for 1 hour before cooking.

Blueberry Jam

Ingredients
1.25 L (5 cups) blueberries
50 mL (1/4 cup) lemon juice
1 L (4 cups) sugar
50 mL (1/4 cup) water
1 170 mL (6 oz) bottle of pectin

Method
— Purée the blueberries in a blender.
— Transfer to a dish; add the lemon juice, sugar and water.
— Cook at 100% for 2 to 3 minutes.
— Let stand for 10 minutes.
— Add the pectin and stir well.
— Cover and store for 24 hours at room temperature before eating.

Level of Difficulty	🍴
Preparation Time	10 min*
Cost per Serving	$
Quantity	approx. 3 cups
Cooking Time	3 min
Standing Time	10 min
Power Level	100%
Write Your Cooking Time Here	

*Let stand 24 hours before eating.

Raspberry Jam

Ingredients
2.5 L (10 cups) raspberries
750 mL (3 cups) sugar
30 mL (2 tablespoons) lemon
juice
175 mL (3/4 cup) water
1 package powdered citrus
fruit pectin

Method
— Purée the raspberries in a
  blender. There should be
  750 mL (3 cups) purée.
— Transfer to a dish, add
  the sugar and lemon juice;
  mix well.
— Cook at 100% for 2 to 3
  minutes; stir.
— Let stand for 10 minutes.
— In a bowl, combine the
  water and pectin.
— Heat at 100% for 30 to 40
  seconds, or until the
  liquid is clear.
— Stir in the raspberries.
— Cover and store for 24
  hours at room
  temperature.
— Transfer to sterilized jars
  and seal.

Level of Difficulty	🍴
Preparation Time	10 min*
Cost per Serving	$
Quantity	approx. 3 cups
Cooking Time	3 min
Standing Time	10 min
Power Level	100%
Write Your Cooking Time Here	

*Let stand 24 hours before eating.

Cherry Jam

Ingredients
625 mL (2-1/2 cups) black
cherries, pitted and crushed
1 L (4 cups) sugar
30 mL (2 tablespoons) lemon
juice
5 mL (1 teaspoon) almond
essence
170 mL (6 oz) bottle of
pectin

Method
— Purée the cherries in a
  blender.
— Transfer to a dish.
— Stir in the sugar, lemon
  juice and almond essence.
— Cover and cook at 100%
  for 2 to 3 minutes.
— Let stand for 10 minutes.
— Add the pectin and stir
  until combined.
— Cover and store for 24
  hours at room
  temperature before eating.

Level of Difficulty	🍴
Preparation Time	15 min
Cost per Serving	$
Quantity	approx. 2 cups
Cooking Time	3 min
Standing Time	10 min
Power Level	100%
Write Your Cooking Time Here	

*Let stand 24 hours before
eating.

Banana Crepes

Ingredients
125 mL (1/2 cup) brown sugar
30 mL (2 tablespoons) butter
juice of 1 lemon
3 bananas, peeled and cut into 2.5 cm (1 in) pieces
125 mL (1/2 cup) whole strawberries
6 crepes
30 mL (2 tablespoons) icing sugar

Method
— Combine the brown sugar, butter and lemon juice.
— Cover and cook at 100% for 1 minute.
— Add the fruits, cover again and continue cooking at 100% for 3 to 4 minutes, stirring once during the cooking time.
— Fill the crepes with the fruit mixture and fold them over.
— Arrange the filled crepes on a plate and sprinkle with icing sugar.
— Heat at 70% for 2 to 3 minutes, giving the dish a half-turn after 1-1/2 minutes.

Level of Difficulty	🍴
Preparation Time	5 min
Cost per Serving	$ $
Number of Servings	6 crepes
Cooking Time	8 min
Standing Time	None
Power Level	100%, 70%
Write Your Cooking Time Here	

Apple Crepes

Ingredients
4 apples
15 mL (1 tablespoon) cinnamon
30 mL (2 tablespoons) Cointreau
125 mL (1/2 cup) brown sugar
15 mL (1 tablespoon) cornstarch
30 mL (2 tablespoons) cold water
6 crepes

Method
— Peel, core and thinly slice the apples; put them in a dish.
— Add the cinnamon, Cointreau and brown sugar.
— Cover and cook at 100% for 4 to 5 minutes, stirring once.
— Remove the apples from the dish and drain in a sieve; reserve the liquid.
— Combine the cornstarch and cold water; add to the reserved liquid.
— Cook at 100% for 1 to 2 minutes, stirring once.
— Fill the crepes with the apple mixture and fold them over.
— Pour the sauce over the crepes and reheat at 70% for 2 to 3 minutes before serving.

Level of Difficulty	🍴
Preparation Time	15 min
Cost per Serving	$
Number of Servings	6 crepes
Cooking Time	10 min
Standing Time	None
Power Level	100%, 70%
Write Your Cooking Time Here	

99

Decorating

If there is one field where the pastry chef can truly give her imagination free reign it is in decoration. As with other foods, some well-known desserts require a classic presentation while others can be more daringly decorated. But in either case, the extra few minutes taken to decorate are always worthwhile.

The ingredients that can be used to decorate a dessert are so numerous that it would be impossible to list them all here. Instead, we will try to give you an idea of what features can contribute to making a dessert even more appetizing. Chocolate in all its forms: sprinkles, shavings, geometric figures cut from a thin sheet, etc., all add panache to many different desserts. Small whole fresh fruits always add that final touch to fruit desserts; make sure to choose the prettiest pieces. Larger fruits can be cut in slices, in quarters, in strips, etc. Candied fruits and nuts are attractive decorations. Larger nuts, like coconuts, should be finely grated. Whole coffee beans and some spices such as cinnamon sticks and cloves add visual interest and flavor to molded desserts and creams. Some fresh herbs, such as mint or sprigs of holly at Christmas time (but don't eat them!) are very decorative. The leaves of some fruits can be attractively arranged on fruit-based desserts, but make sure to wash them in cold water first.

Special attention should be paid to frosted desserts, such as cakes. The frosting can be worked with a spatula or smoothed and decorated with a decorating bag.

You can make pastries, fruit tarts and tartlets appear even more inviting by covering the surface with a transparent glaze.

There are so many things you can do, so trust your imagination. And next time you prepare a dessert don't think of trying to "save time" by neglecting its decoration.

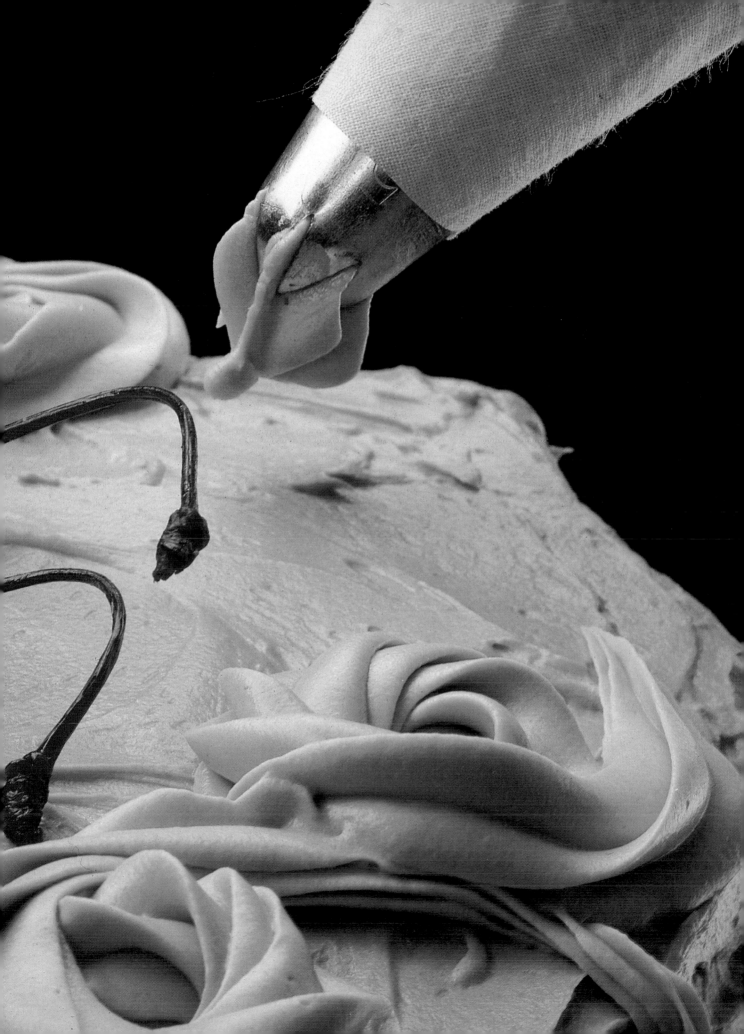

The Decorating Tube: The Pastry Chef's Pen

You have already experimented with a decorating bag and have obtained encouraging results. Bravo! Do you now feel ready to push a little further ahead and try some new ideas? If you do, we suggest you take a close look at some of the possibilities afforded by a set of tubes. We don't expect the following descriptions to limit you. On the contrary! They should be a guide for your next experiments in cake and pastry decorating and allow you to create some unique motifs.

The round tube, available in different sizes, can be used for stringwork, zigzags, dots, beads or spirals. It pipes out the icing in an even strip.

Double and triple tubes are useful for framing a surface by piping out parallel strips of icing or symmetrical dots.

The flat tube produces a ribbon of icing in a straight line. The ribbon can also be arranged in waves.

The scalloped flat tube produces a scalloped ribbon of icing, a little more complex than the previous tube. It is a little more delicate and makes the motifs appear more fragile.

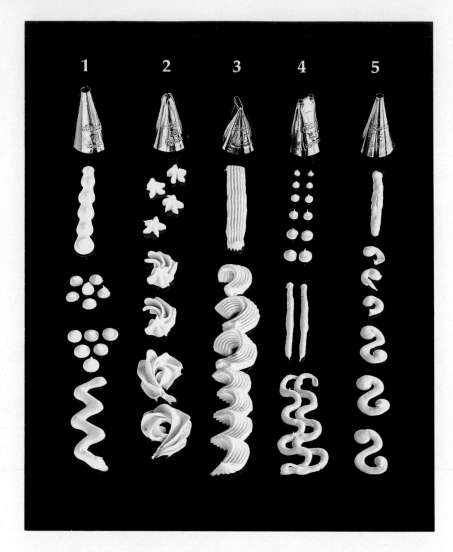

1. **Large round tube**
2. **Star tube**
3. **Scalloped flat tube**
4. **Double tube**
5. **Medium round tube**

Some tubes have a thin, wide opening, making them appropriate for complex motifs but they only make straight lines. The leaf tube does not make only leaves, as its name might suggest. It can also be used to make flower petals or other more imaginative motifs.

The scalloped semi-circular tube is used mainly to create small or large shells. It can also be used to make thick ropes.

The star tube is a multi-purpose tube and probably the most widely used. It can be used for everything from the simplest scalloped line to the most complex design, from small rosettes to large shells.

The flower tube is available in many sizes. As its name suggests, it can be used to form a complete flower on a surface, and also to create charming elaborate motifs.

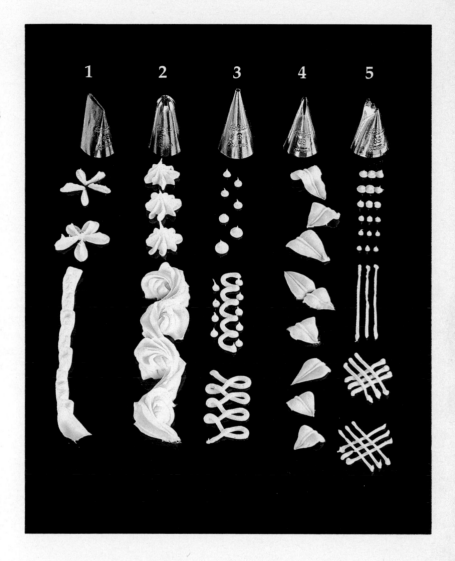

1. **Flat tube**
2. **Star tube**
3. **Small round tube**
4. **Leaf tube**
5. **Triple tube**

Decorating with Chocolate

There is no need to describe the taste of chocolate; it is universally known and loved. As well as being eaten on its own, this mixture of cocoa, butter and sugar is frequently used in pastry- and cake-making, either to flavor a dessert or to decorate it. We will now take a look at this latter use; the incredible possibilities of decorating with chocolate will make any dessert even more appetizing.

Hard Chocolate and Melted Chocolate

In order to decorate with chocolate, it must be transformed. You can grate, slice or chop a piece of hard chocolate or you can melt it and pour it into a mold or cut it in a special shape. In fact there's no reason why you couldn't use part of the chocolate cold and melt another part.

Pieces of **hard chocolate** can easily be transformed into small decorative pieces, baskets or fine strips.

Melted chocolate can also be made into pretty baskets, poured into a mold or cut into many unusual shapes.

MICROTIPS

Adapting Traditional Cake Recipes

Ingredients:
1. When adapting a recipe for the microwave never reduce the quantity of eggs as you would the water or oil.
2. The quantity of sugar can be reduced without unbalancing the chemical compositon of the cake. Of course, reducing the amount of sugar depends on your taste or diet and not on the fact that you are using a microwave oven.
3. If you wish to use whole wheat flour instead of white flour remember that whole wheat flour is heavier: 400 mL (1-2/3 cups) of this flour equals 500 mL (2 cups) white flour.
4. Cake recipes for the microwave generally require more baking powder. However, first try adapting a traditional recipe using the same quantity. If the results are not satisfactory, try reducing the amount of liquid. Increase the amount of baking powder only as a last resort.

Method:
1. Since the time required for microwave cooking is shorter than traditional oven cooking the batter and dough have less time to rise. When adapting a traditional recipe, let the dough stand 5 to 10 minutes before cooking so that the yeast has time to react.
2. Never flour a pan before microwave cooking. Use crumbled graham wafers or breadcrumbs. Better yet, spray the inside of the pan with an anti-stick coating.

Dessert Terminology

Baba: Small cakes made with leavened dough and raisins and soaked in rum or kirsch after baking.

Blanch: Process of removing the papery skins covering nuts, almonds and peanuts by plunging them into boiling water.

Caramelize: Caramel is sugar that has been dissolved in twice its volume of water and cooked until golden brown. You can caramelize sauces and creams by adding caramel to them. Another way to caramelize a dessert is to coat the interior of the pan with caramel, so that it will form a coating when the dessert is turned out. Or you can cover a dessert with sugar and then melt the sugar under the boiler until it caramelize.

Cream: To slowly beat together butter or margarine and sugar to make a fluffy and soft mixture.

Entremets: Historically the term referred to a sweet or savory dish, served with a roast or other main course. Culinary tradition of the time held that all the dishes be served at the same time so that the guest could choose as he wished. Today, the word has a double meaning: light, sweet dish served before the dessert, or sumptuous desserts served at the end of the meal.

Flambé: When a dessert is served flambé, it is first covered with an alcoholic liquor and then served alight.

Genoese: As its name indicates, this light confection is originally from the town of Genoa, in Italy. It is different from other batters in that whole eggs are beaten over hot water in a double boiler. The genoese is very light and delicate and is used as the base for many filled cakes.

Glaze: You glaze a dessert when you give it a glossy finish. There are a variety of glazes, such as syrup, fondant and frosting. A glaze for pastry consists of eggs beaten with either milk or water and brushed on before baking. This type of glaze gives pastry a lovely golden appearance.

Knead: Kneading is the hand process unsed for combining a stiff dough.

Mousse: A smooth light mixture that may be sweet or savory, usually made with beaten egg whites and cream, and sometimes set with gelatin.

Parfait: A rich frozen dessert made with a egg mousse base, flavoring and whipped cream.

Pastry Tube: A cone-shaped utensil attached to a piping bag and used to decorate cakes, pastries, etc. Since the tips of the tubes can be many different shapes, infinite variations in decoration are possible.

Sweetener: A sugary substance (honey, syrup, sugar) used to sweeten a bitter liquid or solid mixture and to soften bitter tastes.

Trifle: An English dessert that combines cake (usually sponge or pound cake), fruit, custard and whipped cream, often flavored with sherry and served in a large glass bowl.

Undercrust: Pastry dough rolled out with a rolling pin to form the base of many desserts.

Whisk: To beat rapidly with a circular motion in order to make a mixture lighter by incorporating air.

Glossary of Culinary Terms

Apples à l'Andalouse: peeled, cored and poached apples; covered with meringue and cooked in the oven. Served with Condé rice.

Apples à Dauphine: apples peeled, cored and cooked in the oven; cooled and served in Condé rice with apricot syrup, flavored with kirsch.

Apples à la Norvégienne: cold poached apples served with vanilla ice cream and covered with lemon cream.

Apricots en chemise: raw apricot halves, sprinkled with sugar, wrapped in chou pastry, brushed with butter and cooked in the oven and sprinkled with powdered sugar before serving.

Blueberries à la Suisse: blueberries marinated in rum and vanilla sugar, served in a glass, garnished with Chantilly cream.

Chantilly Cream: whipped cream flavored with vanilla.

Jalousies: thinly rolled flaky pastry, cut in wide slices, the centre spread with almond paste and garnished with small strips of pastry in a criss-cross pattern. The pastry is cooked in the oven, brushed with apricot jam and cut in pieces.

Condé rice: rice cooked in sugared milk flavored with vanilla.

Conversion Chart

Conversion Chart for the Main Measures Used in Cooking

Volume	
1 teaspoon	5 mL
1 tablespoon	15 mL
1 quart (4 cups)	1 litre
1 pint (2 cups)	500 mL
1/2 cup	125 mL
1/4 cup	50 mL

Weight	
2.2 lb	1 kg (1000 g)
1.1 lb	500 g
0.5 lb	225 g
0.25 lb	115 g
1 oz	30 g

Metric Equivalents for Cooking Temperatures

°C	°F	°C	°F
49°C	120°F	120°C	250°F
54°C	130°F	135°C	275°F
60°C	140°F	150°C	300°F
66°C	150°F	160°C	325°F
71°C	160°F	180°C	350°F
77°C	170°F	190°C	375°F
82°C	180°F	200°C	400°F
93°C	200°F	220°C	425°F
107°C	225°F	230°C	450°F

Readers will note that, in the recipes, we give 250 mL as the equivalent for 1 cup and 450 g as the equivalent for 1 lb and that fractions of these measurements are even less mathematically accurate. The reason for this is that mathematically accurate conversions are just not practical in cooking. Your kitchen scales are simply not accurate enough to weigh 454 g—the true equivalent of 1 lb—and it would be a waste of time to try. The conversions given in this series, therefore, necessarily represent approximate equivalents, but they will still give excellent results in the kitchen. No problems should be encountered if you adhere to either metric or imperial measurements throughout a recipe.

Index